Cambridge Elements ≡

Elements in Behavioural and Experimental Economics
edited by
Nicolas Jacquemet
University Paris-1 Panthéon Sorbonne and the Paris School of Economics

Olivier L'Haridon
Université de Rennes 1

ESTIMATION OF STRUCTURAL MODELS USING EXPERIMENTAL DATA FROM THE LAB AND THE FIELD

Charles Bellemare
Université Laval

CAMBRIDGE
UNIVERSITY PRESS

Shaftesbury Road, Cambridge CB2 8EA, United Kingdom

One Liberty Plaza, 20th Floor, New York, NY 10006, USA

477 Williamstown Road, Port Melbourne, VIC 3207, Australia

314–321, 3rd Floor, Plot 3, Splendor Forum, Jasola District Centre,
New Delhi – 110025, India

103 Penang Road, #05–06/07, Visioncrest Commercial, Singapore 238467

Cambridge University Press is part of Cambridge University Press & Assessment,
a department of the University of Cambridge.

We share the University's mission to contribute to society through the pursuit of
education, learning and research at the highest international levels of excellence.

www.cambridge.org
Information on this title: www.cambridge.org/9781009362634
DOI: 10.1017/9781009362627

First published 2023

A catalogue record for this publication is available from the British Library.

ISBN 978-1-009-36263-4 Paperback
ISSN 2634-1824 (online)
ISSN 2634-1816 (print)

Additional resources for this publication at www.cambridge.org/bellemare

Estimation of Structural Models Using Experimental Data From the Lab and the Field

Elements in Behavioural and Experimental Economics

DOI: 10.1017/9781009362627
First published online: January 2023

Charles Bellemare
Université Laval

Author for correspondence: Charles Bellemare, cbellemare@ecn.ulaval.ca

Abstract: Behavioral economics provides a rich set of explicit models of nonclassical preferences and belief formation that can be used to estimate structural models of decision-making. At the same time, experimental approaches allow the researcher to exogenously vary components of the decision-making environment. The synergies between behavioral and experimental economics provide a natural setting for the estimation of structural models. This Element will cover examples supporting the following arguments: (1) experimental data allow the researcher to estimate structural models under weaker assumptions and can simplify their estimation, (2) many popular models in behavioral economics can be estimated without any programming skills using existing software, (3) experimental methods are useful to validate structural models. This Element aims to facilitate adoption of structural modeling by providing Stata codes to replicate some of the empirical illustrations that are presented. Examples covered include estimation of outcome-based preferences, belief-dependent preferences, and risk preferences.

Keywords: experimental data, structural models, behavioral economics, data analysis, microeconometrics

JEL classifications: C93, D63, D84

ISBNs: 9781009362634 (PB), 9781009362627 (OC)
ISSNs: 2634-1824 (online), 2634-1816 (print)

Contents

1 Introduction   1

2 A Motivating Example   6

3 Estimation Using First-Order Conditions   11

4 Estimation Using Discrete Choice Models   16

5 Uncertainty in Structural Models   33

6 Model Validation   57

7 Conclusion   62

8 Content of Online Appendix   63

References   66

The Online Appendix can be accessed at
www.cambridge.org/bellemare

1 Introduction

Structural models have traditionally been used to perform welfare analysis of policy changes affecting the choice environment of firms and individuals. Because this environment is explicitly modeled along with preferences, beliefs of decision-makers, and constraints, such models can be used to predict the impact of a counterfactual change of the choice environment holding preferences and beliefs constant. Estimation of structural models discussed in this Element begins by first specifying an economic model where a decision-maker is assumed to derive value (omitting subscripts for the time being) $V(c, \mathbf{x}, \boldsymbol{\theta})$ for all alternatives c in their choice set (whether discrete or continuous). Values typically reflect utility, expected utility, etc..., and depend on variables defining the choice environment $\mathbf{x}$ of that decision-maker, as well as on a vector of structural parameters $\boldsymbol{\theta}$. Structural parameters characterize preferences and beliefs when relevant. A statistical model is derived in a second step from $V(c, \mathbf{x}, \boldsymbol{\theta})$ by introducing randomness in some way (see e.g. Section 3.1). Statistical models provide a mapping between the distribution of choices (or moments of this distribution) and the structural parameters $\boldsymbol{\theta}$.[1]

An attractive feature of structural models is that there is no way to hide what is driving the predictions that are generated – preferences, beliefs, constraints, and the choice environment are normally all clearly laid out. The acceptance of structural modeling as a useful empirical approach for inferences on mechanisms driving behavior varies across fields of economics. Keane (2010) paints a somewhat pessimistic view of the future of structural modeling, arguing a decline in adoption can be explained by several key factors. In particular, the first reason he highlights relates to the amount of labor involved in writing a good paper, possibly discouraging young doctoral students and junior professors seeking tenured positions. The second reason concerns the notion that structural modeling requires imposing strong assumptions (behavioral and statistical) relative to simpler reduced-form approaches. Rust (2010) responds to Keane (2010) by arguing that his pessimism is not entirely warranted. While acknowledging that structural work has declined in some areas (public and labor economics in particular), he highlights fields in economics where structural modeling is either commonly accepted (such as industrial organization)

---

[1] Other "structural" models in econometrics focus instead on estimating the causal impact of possibly endogenous explanatory variables on a given outcome variable using reduced-form techniques. In these models, researchers do not specify an economic model in a first step. Rather, they directly specify a statistical model to jointly model the outcome variable and the explanatory variables of interest. These "structural" models are labeled so in many econometric textbooks, often when discussing approaches using instrumental variables (see e.g. Greene, 2003).

or growing and well accepted (judging from publications in top journals), including behavioral economics.

Behavioral economics provides a rich set of explicit models of nonclassical preferences and belief formation which can be estimated using a structural model. At the same time, experimental approaches allow researchers to exogenously vary components of the decision-making environment. The synergy between behavioral and experimental economics provides a natural setting for the estimation of structural models. Importantly, this synergy offers possibilities to reduce the importance of the factors identified by Keane (2010) and which are believed to limit adoption of the approach. In this Element several examples will be provided to highlight the following messages:

1. *Experimental data can be used estimate structural models under weaker assumptions, thereby increasing their credibility.*

Examples will be provided to highlight how computational requirements and thus labor involved in estimating a structural model can be reduced when exploiting experimental data. Intuitively, experiments provide exogenous variation of key variables and thus does not emerge from the behavior of subjects themselves. Such exogenous variation can be exploited to reduce behavioral and distributional assumptions. Absent such data, researchers need to model the possibly endogenous change in key model variables, requiring additional assumptions at various levels. Paarsch and Shearer (1999), for example, estimate a principal agent model using nonexperimental firm-level data. There, incentives are assumed to be endogenously set by the firm on the basis of working conditions and worker outside options. Estimation of the model taking into account this endogeneity involves nonlinear estimation methods. Shearer (2004) estimates the same preference structure for workers using data from a field experiment where incentives are varied exogenously. The model is estimated using simple linear regression methods without assumptions about how the firm sets the level of incentives.

2. *Experimental methods can easily be used to validate structural models.*

In some instances the use of experimental data provides the means to conduct a convincing test of the underlying model structure even without implementing hold-out treatments. Bajari and Hortacsu (2005) validate structural models of bidding behavior in auctions using data from the lab. These models allow to recover the distribution of private valuations of bidders in the auctions analyzed. Distributions of private values are never observed in nonexperimental bidding data. However, these distributions are known to experimenters who use them to assign private values to subjects. Distributions of private values predicted by structural models fitted using experimental data can thus be compared to the experimental distributions used to assign private values to subjects in the experiments. In other instances running new experimental treatments to test implications of an estimated structural model (in the lab and perhaps in the field) is often feasible and almost surely desirable. The benefits of validating a model using data from new experimental treatments in lab or the field provide additional evidence supporting the predictions of a model. Duflo, Hanna, and Ryan (2012), for example, validate a structural model estimated using non-experimental data by comparing the predicted impact of introducing incentives to increase workplace performance with the experimental impact of introducing such incentives in the field.

3. *Many popular models in behavioral economics can be estimated without any programming skills using existing software.*

The scope of this Element is to provide an introductory overview of approaches to estimate and validate structural models using experimental data from either the lab or the field.[2] Examples include estimation of outcome-based preferences (constant elasticity of substitution utility, Fehr and Schmidt [1999], Bolton and Ockenfels [2000]) and belief-dependent preferences (guilt aversion and reciprocity). the paper also discusses estimation of risk and ambiguity preferences. The choice of preferences shape the choice-specific value function $V(c, \mathbf{x}, \theta)$ that is specified in the economic model. Special attention will be devoted to measurement of probabilistic beliefs and expectations which are central to models with uncertainty, and how to incorporate these in structural models through the specification of $V(c, \mathbf{x}, \theta)$. The Element will also discuss different approaches to capture randomness in behavior, leading to the specification of a statistical model. We will consider adding errors to $V(c, \mathbf{x}, \theta)$ (or to a function of $V(c, \mathbf{x}, \theta)$). We will also discuss approaches allowing structural parameters θ to vary with both observable and unobservable characteristics of the decision-maker. Stata codes are provided through the online appendix, a subset of which will be presented and discussed in the main text via text boxes highlighted for this purpose. With the exceptions of models where value functions are not a linear combination of parameters (e.g. risk preferences), most models presented in this Element can be estimated without any programming skills, using basic built-in commands, with minor tweaks. Naturally, other

---

[2] DellaVigna (2018) discusses related issues regarding structural modeling in behavioral economics. He notably covers structural models of present bias which are not covered in the current paper.

or more general structural models can be estimated but doing so will require additional programming. These models (apart from those involving risk and ambiguity) mostly fall outside of the scope of this Element which aims to encourage adoption of the approach by reducing entry barriers as much as possible.

Despite the benefits experimental methods provide to facilitate structural modeling, not all research questions benefit from estimation of a structural model. Put differently, the research question should in general dictate the empirical approach that is followed.[3] With the same data, some research questions may require nonstructural methods while other questions can only be answered by specifying and estimating a structural model. Bellemare and Shearer (2009), for example, analyze the effect of a windfall gain (a gift) of $80 on planter daily productivity in a tree-planting firm based in British Colombia (Canada). Their research question is simple: did the gift increase worker performance and firms profits? A nonstructural approach is sufficient to answer this question. The authors use linear panel data methods to measure heterogeneity of worker response to the gain and compute value to the firm of the heterogenous responses. They find that workers reciprocate by significantly raising their average productivity, but the value of the productivity increase is not sufficient to compensate the value of the gift by the firm. This is a common finding in field experiments on gift-giving: when a significant response is observed, it does not provide sufficient value to the firm to justify gift-giving (see discussion in Bellemare and Shearer [2009]). Bellemare and Shearer (2011) use the *same* data to answer a different yet related question: what type of gifts and under which labor market conditions is gift-giving expected to be profitable in this firm? A structural approach is required to address this question for two reasons. First, extensive experimentation may be too costly and problematic. This is probably more important in the field where the target population (e.g. workers) may start being aware of the experiment and adjust their behavior for reasons unrelated to the treatment manipulation. Second, in some settings, structural model can vary elements not controllable using experiments such as the outside options of workers who take part in an experiment. The model of Bellemare and Shearer (2011) was used to perform counterfactual predictions of the effects of various monetary gifts under both tight or slack labor market conditions, conditions that cannot be varied experimentally. They find that gift-giving can be profitable under slack market conditions and when gifts are

---

[3] See Nevo and Whinston (2010), who make a similar argument in the specific area of industrial organization.

presented to workers in the form of piece-rate increases rather than lump-sum windfall gains.

The current Element focuses on behavioral models that have been estimated using data from laboratory and field experiments. Low and Meghir (2017) provide a complementary and less technical overview of the benefits of combining structural econometric modeling and randomized control experiments. They also emphasize and document synergies that emerge through the combination of methods, including enriching structural models as well as using data from randomized experiments for model validation. One interesting example discussed in Low and Meghir (2017) concerns the analysis of the effects of the PROGRESA experiment, a conditional cash transfer program intended to boost school attendance in rural areas of Mexico. Communities were selected before being randomized to either treatment (immediate program implementation) and control conditions (delayed program implementation). Nonstructural data analysis concluded that PROGRESA successfully increased school attendance of children (see Paul Schultz, 2004). Todd and Wolpin (2006) instead estimate a structural dynamic model of educational attainment using data from control communities alone. They subsequently conduct a counterfactual prediction by reducing the wage in the model by an amount compatible with the cash transfer of the program. The hold-out sample of treated communities was used to validate the predictive power of the model. These applications as well as those discussed in the current Element demonstrate that experimental data, regardless of its nature, can enhance structural modeling and add value to collection of experimental data.

Notation: The notation V_c will sometimes be used interchangeably with $V(c, \mathbf{x}_i, \boldsymbol{\theta})$ to represent the choice-specific value function. This is done to simplify reading and presentation. Subject specific subscripts i will also be added (e.g. V_{ic}) to express variation of the function across subjects. In some cases, $V_{ic}(\boldsymbol{\theta}_i)$ will also be used to emphasize models where structural parameters are allowed to vary (or not) across subjects.

The remainder of the Element is structured as follows. Section 2 presents an example to illustrate the benefits of estimating structural models using experimental data. Section 3 discusses estimating structural models using first-order conditions of an optimization problem. Section 4 discusses estimation of structural models using a discrete choice framework. Section 5 presents models in the presence of risk and uncertainty. This section will also discuss measurement of beliefs and expectations as well as simple approaches to handle potential endogeneity of these variables. Section 6 discusses model validation using experimental data. Section 7 concludes.

2 A Motivating Example

In this section we present an example to demonstrate possible synergies between structural modelling and experimental methods. Consider the following model of worker behavior in response to changes in compensation (see Shearer, 2004). Here, the economic model is based on a value function capturing utility of worker i at period t. This function is modeled by

$$V_{it} = r_{it}y_{it} - C_i(e_{it}),\tag{1}$$

where r_{it} is the piece-rate paid to the worker per unit of daily output y_{it}, and $C_i(e_{it})$ is an increasing convex function capturing cost of effort e_{it}. Here, worker compensation does not include a fixed wage, although adding such a wage to the analysis has no consequences as issues related to worker participation are not considered in the example. Assume that worker output is determined by the multiplicative production function

$$y_{it} = e_{it}s_{it},\tag{2}$$

where s_{it} denotes random factors (e.g. weather conditions) determining worker output which are unrelated to the effort exerted. A useful parametrization of the cost of effort function $C_i(e_{it})$ is

$$C_i(e_{it}) = \kappa_i \frac{\gamma e_{it}^{(\gamma+1)/\gamma}}{(\gamma + 1)},$$

where κ_i is a worker specific productivity parameter and γ captures elasticity of output with respect to the piece-rate. Solving for the optimal effort e_{it}^* of the worker given a piece-rate r_{it}, and replacing optimal effort in the multiplicative production function (2) yields the following expression for optimal worker output

$$y_{it}^* = \frac{(r_{it}s_{it})^{\gamma_i}}{\kappa_i^{\gamma_i}}.\tag{3}$$

Taking natural logs on both sides yields

$$\ln(y_{it}^*) = \gamma_i \ln(r_{it}) - \gamma \ln(\kappa_i) + \gamma \ln(s_{it}).\tag{4}$$

This model can be written as a classical linear panel data regression model with unobserved individual heterogeneity.[4]

---

[4] The model is written as

$$\ln(y_{it}^*) = \alpha_0 + \gamma \ln(r_{it}) + \alpha_i + \epsilon_{it},$$

where $\alpha_0 = \mathbf{E}\left((\gamma + 1)\log(s_{it})\right) - \gamma \log(\kappa_1)$, $\alpha_i = -\gamma \log(\kappa_i) + \gamma \log(\kappa_1)$, and $\epsilon_{it} = (\gamma + 1)$ $\log(s_{it}) - \mathbf{E}\left((\gamma + 1)\log(s_{it})\right)$.

Equally important, the economic model and its structure now transition to a statistical model which can be estimated using appropriate data. This transition follows because the economic model embeds a stochastic term s_{it} capturing randomness in productivity for a given worker, conditional on a given piece-rate r_{it}.

The following observations highlight some of the synergies between structural modeling and experimental data.

Observation 1 (Weaker behavioral assumptions): *Paarsch and Shearer (1999) estimate γ (restricted to the same value for all workers) using payroll data from a tree-planting firm based in British Columbia (Canada). They face a significant endogeneity problem – the firm sets higher piece-rates r_{it} on planting blocks which are relatively harder to plant (lower values of s_{it}). This practice ensures workers accept to work under difficult planting conditions. However, this practice also introduces a negative correlation between planting conditions (s_{it}) and observed piece-rates r_{it}. Paarsch and Shearer (2000) solve this problem by making additional assumptions about how the firm sets r_{it}, namely assuming the piece-rate is set such that the least productive worker in the firm is indifferent between working or the minimal wage (the outside option). Shearer (2004) illustrates how experimental data can be used to estimate γ without assumptions about how the firm sets piece-rates. He randomly assigned piece-rates to workers on different treatment blocks. The randomization ensures that r_{it} varies across workers for a given s_{it}.*

The previous observation underlines the weaker behavioral assumptions that are imposed to estimate the model using experimental data. The following observation focuses on the weaker distributional assumptions that are imposed when estimating the model using experimental data.

Observation 2 (Weaker distributional assumptions): *Paarsch and Shearer (1999) estimate their model using Maximum Likelihood which requires additional distributional assumptions about s_{it}. Experimental data can be used to estimate γ using simple linear regression methods with minimal distributional assumptions (conditional moment restrictions).*

Both observations lead to the specification of a simple linear regression model. The latter can be estimated in Stata using the following command (see code `pamodel.do` in the online appendix).

Principal agent model: Stata example (`pamodel.do`)

```
generate logr = log(r)
regress logy logr if gift == 0, cluster(id)
```

---

r and logy are respectively the independent and dependent variables, and id is a variable identifying the different workers/subjects. Here, clustered standard errors are computed given randomization of piece-rates to workers ensures that r_{it} varies across workers for a given s_{it} as discussed above. The data file `pamodel.dta` associated with the Stata code above contains simulated data of worker response both when monetary gifts are provided, and when they are not. We discuss below an extension of the basic model to capture reciprocal preferences associated with gift-giving. The command line above can be executed using only observations for which no gift was given (hence the variable gift is set to 0 to select these observations).

Observation 3 (Random effects vs Fixed effects): *Experimental data allow researchers to use more efficient estimators. Random assignment of experimental subjects to treatment (assignment of workers to piece-rates in the example above) supports maintaining the assumption that unobserved heterogeneity is independent of treatment. As is well known, fixed-effects estimation is relatively inefficient relative to random-effects estimation under these assumptions. Fixed-effects estimation is justified when researchers believe there could exist a relation between unobserved heterogeneity and treatment assignment. This is possibly more likely in the field where researchers may not have perfect control of the assignment of subjects to treatment (as per the case where assignment is delegated to a third party such as a firm). Shearer (2004), for example, estimates equation (4) using fixed-effects out of an excess of caution. In the latter case, the firm made the final assignment of workers to piece-rates and fixed-effects estimation would capture any bias due to nonrandom assignment of workers to treatment resulting from imperfect treatment assignment.*

A final observation presented below requires an extension of the simple model above. Gift-giving has the potential to be used as an effort-inducing device (e.g. Akerlof, 1982). Numerous laboratory and field experiments have found empirical support for the gift-exchange hypothesis (Fehr, Kirchsteiger, and Riedl, 1993; Gneezy and List, 2006; Bellemare and Shearer, 2009; Kube, Maréchal, and Puppe, 2012). Surprise wage cuts trigger a stronger (negative) response than surprise wage increases (see Kube, Maréchal, and Puppe, 2013). A preferences-based explanation is that negative reciprocity dominates positive reciprocity following a wage increase of similar magnitude. Rabin (1993) models reciprocity by adding a psychological payoff function to the utility function of workers. This psychological payoff function interacts kindness of the firm toward the worker with kindness of the worker toward the firm, Section 5.2 details a specific functional form involving higher-order expectations of workers which captures this idea. In the current example, data on beliefs are assumed not available. The economic model of equation (1) can be extended to capture reciprocity by specifying

$$V_{it} = r_{it}y_{it} - C_i(e_{it}) + \beta \left(y_{it} - y_{it}^{NG} \right) Gift_{it}, \tag{5}$$

where $Gift_{it}$ is the monetary value of the unexpected wage increase or decrease (negative gift) to the worker. Reciprocity is captured by the preference parameter $\beta \geq 0$ multiplying kindness of the worker toward the firm, with nonreciprocal workers characterized by $\beta = 0$. Kindness is modeled as the excess production beyond the level that would otherwise be produced absent a gift (y_{it}^{NG}). Structural parameters are β and γ. Solving for optimal effort and substituting the latter in the production function $y_{it} = e_{it}s_{it}$ yields

$$y_{it} = \left(\frac{[r_{it} + \beta G_{it}]}{\kappa_i} \right)^{\gamma} s_{it}^{\gamma+1}. \tag{6}$$

The model above can be estimated using nonlinear least squares using the natural logarithm of y_{it} as the dependent variable, yielding the following estimating equation

$$\ln(y_{it}) = \alpha_0 + \gamma \log(r_{it} + \beta Gift_{it}) + \alpha_i + \epsilon_{it}, \tag{7}$$

where α_0, α_i, and ϵ_{it} were previously defined (see footnote 4).

Principal agent model - Stata example cntd (`pamodel.do`)

```
nl (logy = {cst} + {gamma}*log(r + {beta}*gift )),
vce(cluster id)
```
- -

Here `nl` invokes nonlinear least squares estimation. Parameters in braces {} are the structural parameters that have been named and are to be estimated. Here, estimation exploits all data in the file provided in the online appendix (`pamodel.dta`). These data include simulated productivity both with and without gifts.

Bellemare and Shearer (2011) estimate the model above using data from a field experiment with 18 workers in a medium-sized tree-planting firm.[5] They report estimates of β_i and γ, where β_i is allowed to vary with observable worker characteristics (this extension of (7) is discussed in Section 3). These estimates can be used in the following exercise.

Observation 4 (Confounding factors): *Structural modeling clarifies possible confounding factors that can explain an observed behavioral response. Inspection of (6) reveals that the effect of a gift (negative or positive) will be impacted by the shape of the cost of effort function (γ). Consider, for example, the following two scenarios: a positive wage gift of $100 and a wage cut of the same amount. Equation (6) can be used to predict the change in average worker productivity with and without either the positive gift or the negative wage cut when evaluated. This prediction is performed for $r_{it} = 0.16$ and using estimated values $\beta = 0.001$ and $\gamma = 0.39$ which are comparable to those reported in Bellemare and Shearer (2011).[6] Importantly, we are keeping the same preference parameter when evaluating the effects of a wage increase and a wage cut – reciprocity β does not vary across both scenarios. In this setting, a wage increase of $100 is predicted to lead to increase average worker productivity by 20.8%, while an unexpected wage cut of $100 is predicted to decrease average worker productivity by 31.7%. It would be tempting to conclude from the observation that a wage cut triggers a stronger behavioral response than a wage increase that positive/negative reciprocity differ. However, the strength of reciprocity (captured by β) is held constant. It turns out that convexity of the cost of effort function is driving the differences in predicted response across both scenarios, not differences reciprocity in the gain/loss domains. The model makes clear proper controls for the cost of effort are necessary in order to infer whether reciprocal preferences in the gain/loss domains are really driving behavior.*

It is important to highlight that a simple linear panel regression with worker specific effects will not properly control for differences in cost of effort across

---

[5] The experiment took place on a large homogeneous planting block. On the second day of planting on the block (a Friday), the firm offered $80 to each planter in addition to their regular piece-rate pay. The gift was formulated as a gift from the firm to the workers. Workers were told the gift was a one-time event and would not be repeated in the future.

[6] The percentage change in expected worker output for a monetary gift of value a is given by

$$\frac{\mathbf{E}\left(y_{it}|r_{it}, G_{it} = a\right)}{\mathbf{E}\left(y_{it}|r_{it}, G_{it} = 0\right)} - 1 = \frac{[r_{it} + \beta a]^\gamma}{r_{it}^\gamma} - 1.$$

workers. To see this, consider the estimating equation of the model above (see equation [7]). Assuming correct model specification, this implies that reduced-form approaches will not be able to separate the preference component (β) from the cost of effort component (γ) which can both explain field evidence reported in the literature. To date, separate structural estimates of reciprocal preferences in both the gain and loss domains have not appeared in the literature.

The simple model above illustrates some of the key advantages experimental data bring to the specification and identification of structural models as well as to their estimation. Not all of these advantages apply to any given model. Also, the structure of the model leads to simple estimating equations where the value of experimental data can be assessed.

With that said, some elements of this structure can be questioned. The assumption about the production function (2), for example, is not innocuous. An alternative would be to consider an additive structure $y_{it} = e_{it} + s_{it}$. Assuming s_{it} remains observed before effort is chosen, first-order conditions and optimal productivity now become

$$e_{it}^* = \left(\frac{r_{it}}{\kappa_i}\right)^{\gamma}$$

$$y_{it} = \frac{r_{it}^{\gamma}}{\kappa_i^{\gamma}} + s_{it}.$$

This yields a nonlinear equation that is substantially more involved to estimate regardless whether experimental data are available or not. Choosing effort before or after observing s_{it} does not change optimal e_{it} when $y_{it} = e_{it} + s_{it}$. With $y_{it} = e_{it}s_{it}$ and ex ante unknown shock s_{it} we get

$$e_{it}^* = \left(\frac{r_{it}\mathbf{E}(s_{it})}{\kappa_i}\right)^{\gamma}.$$

Here again estimation of this extended model is more involved regardless of the type of data used. These examples demonstrate both the benefits and the limitations of using experimental data to enhance structural modeling.

3 Estimation Using First-Order Conditions

In this section we discuss estimation of structural models using first-order conditions of an optimization problem. The use of first-order conditions as a basis for estimation can be motivated on many grounds. First-order conditions of some models are transparent and demonstrate the anticipated impact of the model structure and underlying variables on behavior. The model of gift-giving and reciprocity in the previous section is a good example of this. Compare the utility function (5) with corresponding first-order conditions (7). First-order conditions already convey information on the anticipated confounding effects of the possibly convex cost-of-effort function on responses to a wage increase/decrease even prior to estimation. This information is not readily available by inspecting the utility function (5).

Suppose subject i in an experiment is presented an open-ended question format prompting the subject to choose a value y_i from an interval on the real line. Assume subject i derives value $V(y_i, \mathbf{x}_i, \boldsymbol{\theta})$ given preference parameters $\boldsymbol{\theta}$ and treatment parameters $\mathbf{x}_i$. Here, treatment parameters capture experimental payoffs of subject i, etc. Optimal y_i^* solves the following first-order condition:

$$V'(y_i^*, \mathbf{x}_i, \boldsymbol{\theta}) = 0. \tag{8}$$

The first-order condition approach requires that a closed form expression for y_i^* can be solved from (8), leading to

$$y_i^* = F(\mathbf{x}_i, \boldsymbol{\theta}), \tag{9}$$

where $F(\cdot)$ is derived from the preference structure of $V'(\cdot)$ above. Reduced-form regression equation estimation specifies a functional form for $F(\cdot)$ which is unrelated to the structure of first-order conditions of an optimization problem such as (8). In particular, the reduced-form approach will tend to specify $F(\cdot)$ for data-fitting purposes. As a result, the choice of $f(\cdot)$ and the interpretation of β are related to the preferences and constraints of a structural model.

Equation (9) is deterministic – the model predicts all subjects assigned the same treatment conditions $\mathbf{x}_i$ should choose the same y_i^*. Bringing the model to data requires modeling heterogeneity in behavior for given treatment conditions. We next discuss two main approaches and present examples for each. We then discuss the advantages of combining the two approaches.

3.1 Modeling Behavioral Heterogeneity

3.1.1 Preference Heterogeneity

The main advantage of introducing heterogeneity through structural parameters such as those characterizing preferences of subjects is that these parameters are typically of primary interest to researchers. Recovering this heterogeneity across the subject population is thus a worthwhile endeavor. Doing so requires extending equation (9) to

$$y_i^* = F(\mathbf{x}_i, \boldsymbol{\theta}_i), \tag{10}$$

where $\boldsymbol{\theta}_i$ is now indexed by i. For simplicity, let $\boldsymbol{\theta}_i = \theta_i$ be a scalar preference parameter. A simple model of preference heterogeneity can be written as

$$\theta_i = \mathbf{z}_i \boldsymbol{\theta} + \epsilon_i^{\theta}, \tag{11}$$

where $\mathbf{z}_i$ is a vector of observable characteristics of subject i (gender, age, etc.), the vector $\boldsymbol{\theta}$ captures the importance of these characteristics, and ϵ_i^{θ} represents remaining unobserved preference heterogeneity. The downside of using this approach to capture behavioral heterogeneity is that any behavior deviating from the predictions of the model (allowing for heterogeneity of β_i) is not accounted for, including likely noise in decision-making.

3.1.2 Random Disturbances

Including additive random disturbances to (9) is useful to capture deviations from the model structure specified. A classic example of this approach is Andreoni and Miller (2002), who test whether observed altruistic behavior in dictator games can be rationalized by a well-defined continuous, convex, and monotonic utility function. They exploit a simple laboratory design where subjects in the role of dictators make multiple decisions (8 to 11) on how to share a surplus with other subjects. The design varies the amount of the surplus to be shared and the cost of sharing. They find that 43% of subjects can be exactly classified as having either selfish, Leontief (payoff equalizing), and perfect substitute preferences. Andreoni and Miller (2002) specify and estimate a structural model of altruistic preferences that can best explain behavior of these remaining 57% of subjects. Their economic model is based on the following constant elasticity of substitution utility function defined over the payoffs of dictators (π_i^d) and the payoff of the other subject (π_i^o):

$$V_i = \left[\alpha(\pi_i^d)^{\rho} + (1 - \alpha)(\pi_i^o)^{\rho} \right]^{1/\rho}, \tag{12}$$

where $\sigma = 1/(\rho - 1)$ is the elasticity of substitution between dictator and other subject. Transformed budget constraint is $m = \pi_d + p\pi_p$, with $m = M/p_d$ and $p = p_p/p_d$, where M denotes the budget, (π_p, π_d) are the payoffs of the passive player and the dictator, and (p_p, p_d) are the prices. First-order condition yields

$$\pi_{ig}^d = \frac{\gamma_0}{p^{\gamma_1} + \gamma_0} m_{ig}, \tag{13}$$

where $\gamma_0 = \left(\dfrac{\alpha}{1 - \alpha} \right)^{1/(1-\rho)}$ and $\gamma_1 = -\dfrac{\rho}{1 - \rho}$ are deduced from parameters (γ_0, γ_1) to be estimated in a first step. To proceed with estimation, an error term is added to (13), yielding a statistical model which is estimated by Maximum Likelihood to take into account censoring at either end of the budget constraint. Structural parameters can be recovered in a second step using

$$\rho = \frac{\gamma_1}{\gamma_1 - 1}, \qquad \sigma = (\gamma_1 - 1), \qquad \alpha = \frac{1}{1 + \gamma_0^{1/(\gamma_1 - 1)}},$$

where (γ_0, γ_1) by first-step estimates. Standard errors of estimated structural parameters can be computed using the delta method (see e.g. Greene, 2018).[7]

Note that Andreoni and Miller (2002) build their statistical model by an error term which does not originate from the first-order conditions of the economic model (13). This differs from randomness in the principal agent model outlined in Section 2 where part of the randomness originated from the production function that is present in the economic model.

3.1.3 Combining Preference Heterogeneity and Random Disturbances

It is often limiting to focus exclusively on either preference heterogeneity or random disturbances to bring the model to the data. First, preference heterogeneity is a robust observation in laboratory and field experiments alike. Second, not allowing for random disturbances outside the limits imposed by the structure imposes restrictions on the type of data patterns the model can accommodate. Departures capture possible unobserved preferences and deviations from the model that is specified and estimated. A more general approach is to combine preference heterogeneity and random disturbances when possible.

Bellemare and Shearer (2011) adopt a combined approach to estimate a model of reciprocity in the firm presented in Section 2. The natural logarithm of (6) leads to the following regression equation

$$\log(y_{it}) = \gamma \log(r_{it} + \beta_i G_{it}) - \gamma \log(\kappa_i) + (\gamma + 1)\log(s_{it}),$$

where heterogenous values of the reciprocity parameter β_i are modeled. Let x_{it} denote an observable covariate and define $\beta_i = \beta_0 + \beta_1 x_{it}$.

$$\log(y_{it}) = \alpha_0 + \gamma \log(r_{it} + \beta_0 G_{it} + \beta_1 G_{it} x_{it}) + \alpha_i + \varepsilon_{it}. \tag{14}$$

It follows that (7) is a special case when $\beta_1 = 0$ in (14) above. It is straightforward to implement his extension as the following example shows.

Principal agent model - Stata example cntd (`pamodel.do`)

```
nl (logy = cst + gamma*log(r + beta0*gift +
beta1*gift*x)), vce(cluster id)
```

---

[7] Andreoni and Miller (2002) do not report standard errors for the estimated structural parameters. The file **altruism.do** in the online appendix implements the two-step estimation of the structural parameters of this model.

Here, the reciprocity parameter is allowed to vary with respect to a covariate x (gender, age, tenure). The effects of additional covariates can be measured by simply adding additional interaction effects with the `gift` variable.

Bellemare and Shearer (2011) did not consider heterogeneity of (γ_i), although this extension poses no real challenges as long as there exists independent variation of r_{it} and multiple decisions per subjects are observed. A simple way to incorporate this heterogeneity is to specify $\gamma_i = \gamma_0 + \gamma_1 x_{ij} + \eta_i$ where $\eta_i \sim h(\boldsymbol{\eta})$.[8]

3.2 Discreteness of Choice Data and the First-Order Condition Approach

While the experimental design may theoretically allow to collect data on continuous choice variables y_i^*, observed choices are typically very discrete. One such example is given by Cappelen et al. (2007), who analyze the distribution of the share of surplus subjects in the role of dictators keep for themselves. In their experiment, dictators were asked to make decisions using an open-ended question format prompting them to distribute a surplus (in Norwegian kroner, NOK) between themselves and another player. The authors begin by presenting a fairness model (a utility function) and corresponding first-order conditions. These conditions have the form

$$y_i^* = F_i(\mathbf{x}_i, \boldsymbol{\theta}_i). \tag{15}$$

Note that the function $F_i(\cdot)$ in (15) above is now indexed by i to capture one of three fairness ideals considered by the authors.[9] Their first-order conditions are simple, elegant, and easy to interpret. As a result, estimation of the model parameters using these conditions would appear natural. Nevertheless, estimation of the model was conducted using a discrete choice approach (a random utility model, see Section 4). The approach chosen was motivated by the following observation. Theoretically, there was no restriction on the numerical values subjects could choose to determine the share of their surplus to distribute. In practice, Cappelen et al. (2007) note that their observed choice data are very coarse – 184 of the 190 proposed offers of dictators were multiples of NOK 100, while the remaining 6 offers were multiples of NOK 50. Also, there is

---

[8] The special case with $\eta_i \sim N(0, \sigma^2)$ can be estimated using **xtmixed** in STATA. See the Stata file `pamodel.do` in the online appendix for an example.

[9] These fairness ideals are labeled egalitarianism, libertarianism, or liberal egalitarianism. Each fairness ideal is captured using a different function of the payoffs of each pair of players ($\mathbf{x}_i$).

sizeable selfishness (31% of offers provided nothing to the other player) as well as payoff-equalizing offers (27% of offers). Their structural model can capture some of the discreetness – allowing for three distinct fairness ideals helps to explain some bunching at focal choices compatible with these ideals. Also, they capture unobserved heterogeneity using a continuous distribution for one of their other preference parameters (an element of θ_i in the notation above). However, adding an additional continuous random disturbance to (15) to estimate the model would do little to capture the remaining coarseness in the data. The choice of Cappelen et al. (2007) to estimate their model using a discrete choice model has drawn some criticism in the literature. Conte and Moffatt (2014) revisit estimation of the model using data from Cappelen et al. (2007). The view defended in Conte and Moffatt (2014) is that the choice of design (open-ended response format in the case of Cappelen et al. [2007]) should dictate the modeling approach (basing estimation around first-order conditions in the example above).

4 Estimation Using Discrete Choice Models

It is fair to say that the discrete choice approach is the most popular to estimate structural models in behavioral economics. The attractiveness of the discrete choice approach is explained by various considerations. First, structural models do not always yield first-order conditions that are either easily interpretable or easy to use in order to recover estimates of the model parameters. This was not the case of the gift-exchange model discussed in the previous section. There, the utility function (5) provided fewer insights than first-order conditions (7) into the confounding effect of cost-of-effort on responses to positive/negative gifts. In this section we will cover models where inspection of the specified preferences (i.e. a utility function) is often sufficient to grasp how behavior is predicted to be driven by them. Also, many experimental designs require that subjects make discrete choices, and thus adopting a discrete choice approach to recover estimates of a structural model is often natural.

This section will present prominent behavioral models which can be estimated using a discrete choice approach. The presentation builds on the random utility framework which is one of the most popular approaches to estimate models using discrete choice data. We begin by first presenting the basic random utility framework before extending this framework to capture additional heterogeneity in the model structure (preferences in particular). As will be seen, estimation of many popular models in behavioral economics is possible using built-in estimation commands available in most statistical software. The section will also discuss important experimental design considerations which are necessary to implement in order to capture specific model features, notably unobserved heterogeneity.

The random utility framework with preference heterogeneity presented below relates to the approach of combining preference heterogeneity and random disturbances previously discussed Section 3 which covered estimation using first-order conditions. As we will see, such a combination can be used to capture richer patterns of heterogeneity in the data relative to either a basic random utility framework with no preference heterogeneity, or a framework where preference heterogeneity is the only source of randomness captured by the model. An example of the latter is the approach of Cox, Friedman, and Gjerstad (2007). They propose a framework where the distribution of preferences is parameterized an used to derive discrete choice probabilities for various popular experimental games where reciprocity and fairness likely play an important role.

4.1 Basic Random Utility Framework

We first consider a basic random utility framework where subject i is required to make a choice from a discrete set of J alternatives. Subjects are assumed to derive value V_{ij} for each alternative $j = 1, 2, 3, ...J$ in the set. Values V_{ij} can represent utility, expected utility, or any other preference functional. Researchers further specify the following additive value function:

$$V_{ij} = \mathbf{x}_{ij}\boldsymbol{\theta}, \tag{16}$$

where V_{ij} is assumed for now to be linear in the observable characteristics x_{ij}. The latter typically include monetary payoffs of relevant subjects in an experiment (see examples below). These characteristics can also include individual beliefs to capture behavior when agents and face some degree of uncertainty or risk either about payoffs, the behavior of others, or the beliefs of others. It is assumed for now that these variables enter linearly in (16). Models of risk and ambiguity aversion discussed in Section 5.2 are important examples where such linearity is violated. Finally, we begin by restricting the vector of model parameters θ to be the same across all subjects. This restriction will be relaxed in Section 4.2.

Subjects should is principle select the alternative associated with the highest value V_{ij}. In practice, randomness needs to be accounted for given not all subjects in a given experimental setting (i.e. a given $\mathbf{x}_{ij}$) will choose the same alternative. By symmetry with the estimation of models using first-order conditions discussed previously (Section 3), randomness can be introduced either through preference heterogeneity or random disturbances (or both). The basic random utility model (RUM) captures randomness in choices by introducing random disturbances. We discuss later how to additionally introduce preference heterogeneity by allowing θ to vary across subjects in a given population. This leads to a specification where subjects are now assumed to select an alternative from the set that maximizes the value function including errors:

$$\tilde{V}_{ij} = V_{ij} + \lambda \varepsilon_{ij}$$
$$= \mathbf{x}_{ij}\theta + \lambda \varepsilon_{ij},$$

where ε_{ij} denotes an alternative specific random disturbance while λ is a noise parameter which quantifies the importance of the random disturbances relative to the scale of values V_{ij} of each alternative. These disturbances are sometimes referred to as Fechner errors (Fechner, 1860). These errors can be interpreted as (i) errors in decision-making and/or (ii) unobserved preferences. Disentangling errors from unobserved preferences is in general difficult without additional data. More importantly, they capture specific deviations from maximization behavior. In particular, the noise will dominate differences in valuations V_{ij} when the latter are small and the subject is close to indifferent between the alternatives in the choice set. This implies that such errors cannot capture all possible types of noise in the data. Consider experimental designs where subjects are presented a menu of choices. One famous example is the elicitation of risk preferences presented in Holt and Laury (2002). There, subjects are presented a menu of 10 binary choices between lottery pairs which vary payoff risks. The menu is structured such that subjects should begin favoring one of the lotteries before "switching" and opting for the other lottery as risks vary. Fechner errors capture noise near the switchpoint of each subject. As such, these errors could not account for multiple switchpoints which would occur if some subjects appear to choose randomly across the 10 decision situations. Noise of the latter form is best captured by incorporating a tremble parameter ω in the model. This tremble parameter represents the probability that a subject "trembles" in any given decision situation and selects randomly with equal probability among the available alternatives. Importantly, the probability of a tremble occurring is unrelated to the differences in valuations V_{ij} across j. This means that incorporating a tremble allows the model to capture a fixed quantity of noise in the data across all decision situations, not just decisions situations where subjects are near indifferent between the available alternatives. Tremble and Fechner errors can both be included in a given model, with numerous applications measuring risk preferences doing so (see e.g. Conte, Hey, and Moffatt, 2011; Von Gaudecker, Van Soest, and Wengstrom, 2011). In these papers, the scales of both errors are separately identified by the different noise patterns present in the data. Tremble parameters have also been introduced to capture noise in decision-making in other experimental settings (e.g. Bardsley and Moffatt, 2007).

Consider now application of the basis RUM framework to the analysis of responder behavior in the ultimatum game. Proposers in this game offer responders a discrete share of an amount Π. Responders decide either to accept ($j = a$) or reject ($j = r$) the offer. We start by assuming we observe a single decision for each responder. We assume that the utility of each alternative is given by

$$\tilde{V}_{ia} = V_{ia} + \lambda \varepsilon_{ia}$$
$$= \mathbf{x}_{ia}\theta + \lambda \varepsilon_{ia}$$
$$\tilde{V}_{ir} = V_{ir} + \lambda \varepsilon_{ir}$$
$$= \mathbf{x}_{ir}\theta + \lambda \varepsilon_{ir},$$

where $\mathbf{x}_{ij}$ are the alternative specific explanatory variables. The basic RUM implies that responders are assumed to choose the option $j \in \{a, r\}$ that maximizes their value functions with error:

$$\tilde{V}_{ij} = V_{ij} + \lambda \epsilon_{ij}. \tag{17}$$

A classical parametric assumption used for estimation is to specify ε_{ij} as i.i.d. draws from an extreme-value Type 1 distribution with variance $\pi^2/6$ (see Train, 2009). The variance of ϵ_{it} in the case of extreme value errors is $\pi^2/6$, such that λ allows the variance of unobserved part of the value function to differ from this know constant when fitting the data. The mean of these errors is not zero but is constant across alternatives j, hence the mean of the differences in errors between any two alternatives in the choice set is zero, which leads to the following Conditional Logit formula:

$$\Pr(y_i = a | \mathbf{x}_i) = \frac{\exp\left(\frac{\mathbf{x}_{ia}\theta}{\lambda}\right)}{\exp\left(\frac{\mathbf{x}_{ia}\theta}{\lambda}\right) + \exp\left(\frac{\mathbf{x}_{ir}\theta}{\lambda}\right)}. \tag{18}$$

Here, $\lambda = 0$ implies here that *all* players should either accept or reject a given offer.

A RUM imposes a cardinal representation of utility by construction (see Batley, 2008) for a clear exposition of this point. This does not mean that the scale parameter can be estimated in all RUM, despite their general cardinal properties. It is well known that θ and λ cannot all be identified and estimated (see Train, 2009). In particular, inspection of 18 reveals that scaling up (θ, λ) by a common factor does not alter the choice probability. Hence, there is a infinite combination of the model parameters that can explain equally well the choice data (the choice probabilities). In practice, a normalization needs to be imposed. The estimation of the scale parameter is related to the normalization of utility that is undertaken.

It is common in discrete choice models to normalize utility by setting $\lambda = 1$ and estimate the other remaining parameters. It turns out that this normalization is counterproductive for estimation of many models in behavioral economics. Most of the examples presented below refer to theoretical models where V_{ij} is normalized to the numéraire. Consider the following example applied to responders in the ultimatum game:

Example: Assume responders in the ultimatum game have Fehr and Schmidt (1999) preferences. The value of accepting a given offer in the game is given by:

$$V_{ia} = \pi_{ia} - \alpha \max(0, \Pi - 2\pi_{ia}) - \beta \max(0, 2\pi_{ia} - \Pi)$$
$$= \mathbf{x}_{ia}\theta,$$

such that

$$\mathbf{x}_{ia} = [\pi_{ia}, \max(0, \Pi - 2\pi_{ia}), \max(0, 2\pi_{ia} - \Pi)]$$
$$\theta = (1, -\alpha, -\beta)'.$$

Note that $V_{ir} = 0$ in the ultimatum game. Fehr and Schmidt (1999) present a distribution of (α, β) chosen to broadly match the distributions of offers by sellers and acceptance rates by buyers across a large number of published studies they reference. A natural endeavor is to estimate these parameters and relate them to the distribution presented in the original paper. This requires normalizing utility to the numéraire, setting the coefficient of own payoffs π_{ia} to 1. Doing so allows λ to be estimated freely given the scale of utility has already been determined. Also, preferences parameters under such a normalization allow to place a price on tradeoffs subjects face in a given choice situation. In the example above, (α, β) capture the willingness-to-pay to reduce disadvantageous/advantageous inequity by one unit of currency.

Estimation commands which implement Conditional Logit estimation do not always allow researchers to restrict a coefficient to 1 while at the same time freeing up the scale parameter λ.[10] This may prevent direct estimation of the structural parameters of interest. The direct approach would require programming the likelihood function and estimating the model parameters in a

---

[10] Stata, for example, offers the "constraint" option which can be used to fix parameter values of a chosen explanatory variable to a given value. However, this command does not free up a noise parameter such as λ.

single step. There is, however, a simple two-step indirect approach which does not require programming the likelihood function.

Most statistical software normalize valuations by setting $\lambda = 1$. Under this normalization, the choice probabilities are given by

$$\Pr(y_i = a|\mathbf{x}_i) = \frac{\exp\left(\mathbf{x}_{ia}\widetilde{\theta}\right)}{\exp\left(\mathbf{x}_{ia}\widetilde{\theta}\right) + 1}, \tag{19}$$

where $\widetilde{\theta}$ denotes the vector of reduced-form parameters under this normalization. Reduced-form parameters relate to the structural parameters by the following identities:

$$\widetilde{\theta} = [\theta_1, \theta_2, \theta_3]$$
$$= [1/\lambda, \alpha/\lambda, \beta/\lambda].$$

Given estimates of $\widetilde{\theta} = [\theta_1, \theta_2, \theta_3]$, it is thus possible to recover structural parameters using

$$\lambda = \frac{1}{\theta_1}, \alpha = \frac{\theta_2}{\theta_1}, \beta = \frac{\theta_3}{\theta_1}, \tag{20}$$

where population parameters are replaced by corresponding estimates. Standard errors (more generally elements of covariance matrix of estimated structural parameters) can be computed using the delta method or by simulation using the estimated variance-covariance matrix of the estimated reduced-form parameters.[11] Importantly, the indirect approach does not lead to a loss of efficiency relative to the direct approach. As such, the indirect approach is useful because of its simplicity and because it does not involve having to program the likelihood function of the structural model.

Example: Consider the following simple specification of the value function to capture distributional concerns (see Bolton and Ockenfels, 2000)

$$V_{ij} = \pi_{ij} - \phi\left(\pi_{ij} - 0.5\right)^2 \tag{21}$$
$$= \mathbf{x}_{ij}\theta,$$

where

$$\mathbf{x}_{ij} = \left[\pi_{ij}, \left(\pi_{ij} - 0.5\right)^2\right]$$
$$\theta = (1, -\phi)'.$$

Again, both the direct and indirect approaches can be used to recover estimates of the structural parameters.

---

[11] Standard errors can be calculated using the delta method via the **nlcom** command in Stata.

Our final example is taken from Charness and Rabin (2002). In a two-player game setting, they model value of a given alternative using:

$$V_{ij} = (1 - \rho r_{ij} - \sigma s_{ij} - \theta q_{ij})\pi_{ij} + (\rho r_{ij} + \sigma s_{ij} + \theta q_{ij})\pi_{-ij}$$
$$= \mathbf{x}_{ij}\theta,$$

where

$$\mathbf{x}_{ij} = \left[\pi_{ij}, r_{ij}\pi_{ij}, s_{ij}\pi_{ij}, q_{ij}\pi_{ij}, r_{ij}\pi_{-ij}, s_{ij}\pi_{-ij}, q_{ij}\pi_{-ij}, \right]$$
$$\theta = (1, -\rho, -\sigma, -\theta, \rho, \sigma, \theta)',$$

where r_{ij} and s_{ij} are binary variables taking a value of 1 when $\pi_{ij} > \pi_{-ij}$ and $\pi_{ij} < \pi_{-ij}$ respectively. The variable q_{ij} is also binary and takes the value of 1 if the matched player $(-i)$ previously misbehaved (if applicable to the decision setting). Variables (r_{ij}, s_{ij}, q_{ij}) can all be constructed using the payoffs of players as well as past behavior of player $-i$. Again, valuations (utility) are normalized to the numéraire, freeing up possible estimation of λ.[12]

RUM with Fehr and Schmidt (1999) preferences: Stata example (`discrete.do`)

```
clogit y offer lessneg moreneg, group(decision)
nlcom lambda: 1/_b[offer]
nlcom alpha: _b[lessneg]/_b[offer]
nlcom beta: _b[moreneg]/_b[offer]
```

The matching datafile (`responder.dta`) contains simulated acceptance/rejection decision of responders in the ultimatum game. Section 4.3 describes in detail the simulation. The `clogit` command invokes Conditional Logit estimation (see (19)) and takes as argument the choice variable y, the offers presented to responders `offer`, and the two variable measuring inequity to having less (`lessneg`) and to having more (`moreneg`) than the proposer for the given offer. Output from `clogit` provides the first step reduced-form estimates of $\widetilde{\theta}$ under the normalization $\lambda = 1$. The `nlcom` command uses the reduced-form estimates from the `clogit` command to compute structural estimates using (20), where standard errors are computed using the Delta method.

---

[12] Charness and Rabin (2002) report estimates of this basic RUM (see their Table VI).

4.2 Random Utility Model with Preference Heterogeneity

Part of heterogeneity in behavior in a given treatment condition possibly reflects preference heterogeneity, implying that θ_i varies across i. In the Fehr and Schmidt (1999) example of the previous subsection, $\theta_i = (\alpha_i, \beta_i)$ would apply, meaning that subjects have differing levels of inequity aversion to own and to others' disadvantage. Fehr and Schmidt (1999) present a distribution of (α_i, β_i) generated to match choice probabilities in a collection of published experimental papers. This distribution suggests there is considerable heterogeneity in inequity aversion of subjects across numerous experimental data sets.

It is often desirable to decompose preference heterogeneity in a part that can be explained by observable individual characteristics and a residual part capturing unobserved heterogeneity. It is not uncommon to find that the part of heterogeneity due to unobservables is larger than the part that can be explained by observable characteristics.[13] Importantly, capturing observable heterogeneity is often straightforward whereas approaches to capture unobserved heterogeneity are more varied. We consider first incorporating unobserved preference heterogeneity and later discuss additionally controlling for observable heterogeneity.

Three main approaches have been used in behavioral economics to capture unobserved heterogeneity, namely a parametric approach and two nonparametric approaches (finite mixture and individual-level estimation). We discuss each in turn.

Parametric approach: the population distribution $f(\theta_i)$ of θ_i is assumed known up to a finite vector of parameters. To illustrate, assume that α_i and β_i of the Fehr and Schmidt (1999) model are jointly normally distributed as follows:

$$\alpha_i = \alpha + u_i^\alpha \text{ where } u_i^\alpha \sim N(0, \sigma_\alpha^2) \tag{22}$$

$$\beta_i = \beta + u_i^\beta \text{ where } u_i^\beta \sim N(0, \sigma_\beta^2), \tag{23}$$

where (α, β) capture the respective average disutility from having less and more, σ_α^2 and σ_α^2 are the corresponding population variances, and $N(c, d)$ denotes the normal distribution with mean c and variance d. Of particular interest is to capture correlation between (α_i, β_i). Correlation is relevant if subjects with higher disutility from having less also have (say) higher disutility from having more. The parametric approach can be used to capture preference

---

[13] See, for example, Von Gaudecker, Van Soest, and Wengstrom (2011) for a decomposition of noise and risk preferences between observable and unobservable characteristics.

heterogeneity in a very parsimonious way, involving the estimation of a limited set of five parameters including correlation between α_i and β_i in the example above.

We would ideally like to directly estimate the model parameters. Again, direct estimation of this model is not often possible using standard estimation functions given the scale normalization of value functions that is often used as a default ($\lambda = 1$). It is possible to extend the two-step indirect approach outlined in the previous subsection in the following way. First, estimate the following reduced-form specification with parametric preference heterogeneity: $\widetilde{\boldsymbol{\theta}}_i = (\theta_1, \theta_{2i}, \theta_{3i})$, where

$$\theta_{2i} = \theta_2 + u_i^{\theta_2} \text{ where } u_i^{\theta_2} \sim \mathcal{N}(0, \sigma_{\theta_2}^2)$$

$$= \frac{\alpha}{\lambda} + \frac{u_i^{\alpha}}{\lambda} \text{ where } \frac{u_i^{\alpha}}{\lambda} \sim N\left(0, \frac{\upsilon_{\alpha}^2}{\lambda^2}\right)$$

$$\theta_{3i} = \theta_3 + u_i^{\theta_3} \text{ where } u_i^{\theta_3} \sim \mathcal{N}(0, \sigma_{\theta_3}^2)$$

$$= \frac{\beta}{\lambda} + \frac{u_i^{\beta}}{\lambda} \text{ where } \frac{u_i^{\beta}}{\lambda} \sim N\left(0, \frac{\sigma_{\beta}^2}{\lambda^2}\right).$$

Structural parameters can be recovered using the following identities

$$\lambda = \frac{1}{\theta_1}, \alpha = \frac{\theta_2}{\theta_1}, \beta = \frac{\theta_3}{\theta_1}, \sigma_{\alpha}^2 = \frac{\sigma_{\theta_2}^2}{\theta_1^2}, \sigma_{\beta}^2 = \frac{\sigma_{\beta}^2}{\theta_1^2}. \tag{24}$$

Again, standard errors can be computed using the delta method or by simulation using the estimated variance-covariance matrix of the estimated reduced-form parameters. Note that $Corr(u_i^{\theta_2}, u_i^{\theta_3}) = Corr(u_i^{\alpha}, u_i^{\beta})$. Simulation methods are typically used to estimate discrete choice models using this parametric approach. The numerical complexity associated with estimation is greatly reduced under the additional assumption that ε_{ij} which are added to the value function of each choice alternative (see Section 4.1) are i.i.d. draws from an extreme-value Type 1 distribution. This leads to estimation of a Mixed Logit model (see Train [2009] for more details about estimation). An alternative would be to assume that ε_{ij} are jointly normally distributed, leading to a Multinomial Probit model. In contrast to the Mixed Logit model, estimation of the Multinomial Probit model with preference heterogeneity can be significantly more complex when the size of the choice set increases. Importantly, McFadden and Train (2000) show that the computationally simpler Mixed Logit model can approximate well any RUM with preference heterogeneity, explaining its popularity in empirical applications. It should be noted that the two-step indirect approach is limited here by the fact that the heterogeneity of the noise parameter λ is not allowed. Allowing for such heterogeneity would likely involve direct programming of the statistical model. Individual-level estimation using the two-step indirect approach (see discussion below) avoids these complications, allows for individual specific noise levels and does not require programming.

Mixed Logit with Fehr and Schmidt (1999) preferences - Stata example (`discrete.do`)

```
cmxtmixlogit y offer, random(lessneg moreneg,
correlated) noconstant
nlcom lambda: 1/_b[offer]
nlcom mean_alpha: _b[lessneg]/_b[offer]
nlcom mean_beta: _b[moreneg]/_b[offer]
nlcom var_alpha: _b[Normal:sd(lessneg)]^2/_b[offer]^2
nlcom var_beta: _b[Normal:sd(moreneg)]^2/_b[offer]^2
```

The `cmxtmixlogit` command invokes Mixed Logit estimation when multiple decisions per subject are available. The call to this function takes as argument the choice variable y, the offers presented to responders `offer`, and the two variable measuring inequity to having less (`lessneg`) and to having more (`moreneg`) than the proposer for the given offer. Placing these variables in the `random()` command option allows their effects to vary randomly across subjects following a user-specified parametric distribution (default uses the normal distribution, see StataCorp LLC [2021]), and `correlated` allows distributions to be correlated (in the latter case distributions are restricted to be normally distributed). Output from `cmxtmixlogit` provides the first step reduced-form estimates of $\widetilde{\theta}_i$ under the normalization $\lambda = 1$. The `nlcom` commands use these reduced-form estimates to compute structural estimates using (24), where standard errors are computed using the Delta method.

The main limitation of the parametric approach is that the chosen distribution inevitably imposes restrictions on behavior that may not always be plausible. A joint normal distribution may not sufficiently restrict the support of θ_i (e.g. to impose sign restrictions) to be in perfect concordance with a given behavioral theory. Alternative parametric distributions can nevertheless be used. Bellemare, Kröger, and Van Soest (2008a), for example, use the joint log-normal distribution to impose nonnegativity restrictions on the Fehr and Schmidt (1999) inequity aversion parameters. Cappelen et al. (2007) use the log-normal distribution to impose nonnegativity of the weight subjects place on their fairness ideals relative to self-interest. The log-normal distribution can however have thick tails which could generate predicted parameter values that may seem implausible. On the other hand, the parametric approach often yields simple and parsimonious models, involving few additional parameters to estimate, and can be implemented using standard econometric software.[14]

Additionally capturing observable heterogeneity is relatively straightforward. Consider the following extension of (22) and (23):

$$\alpha_i = z_i\alpha + u_i^\alpha \text{ where } u_i^\alpha \sim \mathcal{N}(0, \sigma_\alpha^2) \tag{25}$$

$$\beta_i = z_i\beta + u_i^\beta \text{ where } u_i^\beta \sim \mathcal{N}(0, \sigma_\beta^2), \tag{26}$$

where z_i is a vector of observable characteristics. This vector will in general contain socio-demographic variables (e.g. age, gender) but could also contain role specific or treatment specific dummy variables.

It is of interest to ask whether ignoring preference heterogeneity and estimating a Conditional Logit model (see (18)) will recover estimates of the mean value of θ_i (or some other measure of central tendency). Train (1998) compares preferences of fish anglers estimated using a Conditional Logit model (restricting preference parameters to be the same across individuals) with those of various Mixed Logit models (with normally or log-normally distributed parameters). He finds that inferences from Conditional Logit estimates differ from those of Mixed Logit models when the latter allows for correlation between the preference parameters (as in the Fehr and Schmidt [1999] example above). Other papers also report differences between estimated preferences taking or not heterogeneity into account (see Revelt and Train, 1998). Section 4.3 presents a simulation exercise comparing estimates ignoring or not preference heterogeneity in the Fehr and Schmidt (1999) model. Results presented there also suggest that estimates ignoring heterogeneity will likely diverge from the population averages estimated using Mixed Logit (allowing for random preferences) as well as from true population averages used in the simulation.

Finite-mixture approach: The finite mixture approach does not impose that $f(\theta_i)$ belongs to a parametric family. Under the finite mixture approach, each subject belongs to a class k defined by a common parameter vector θ_k. For the Fehr and Schmidt (1999) model, a finite mixture would be represented as:

---

[14] Stata code and data implementing this model are discussed in Section 4.3.

$$f(\alpha_i, \beta_i) = \omega_1 \text{ if } (\alpha_i, \beta_i) = (\alpha_1, \beta_1)$$
$$= \omega_2 \text{ if } (\alpha_i, \beta_i) = (\alpha_2, \beta_2)$$
$$\vdots$$
$$= \omega_K \text{ if } (\alpha_i, \beta_i) = (\alpha_K, \beta_K),$$

where ω_k presents the share of subjects in class k, with shares summing to 1 ($\sum_{k=1}^{K} \omega_k = 1$). The number of classes K is an unknown population parameter. However, the discrete nature of this parameter prevents its estimation alongside other parameters of the model. In most applications of finite mixtures, a model is repeatedly estimated by increasing the number of classes, and information criteria (AIC and BIC) that trade-off model fit (the log-likelihood function value evaluated at the model estimates) and number of estimated model parameters are computed to determine the optimal number of classes (see Train, 2008). The performance of AIC and BIC to identify the number of classes is mixed and briefly reviewed in Section 6). The finite mixture approach is thus more flexible than the parametric approach but will in general require programming and may become numerically unstable as the number of classes increases.

A recent application of the finite mixture approach is provided by Bruhin, Fehr, and Schunk (2019). They implement a series of binary choice dictator games varying advantageous and disadvantageous inequity between both players. These games identify aversion to having more and less respectively. They also implement reciprocity games, adding a kind or unkind move by one of the players to the earlier dictator games. These games additionally identify the effects of positive/negative reciprocity. They specify a random utility model where preferences extend those of Charness and Rabin (2002) (see Section 4.1) to measure both positive and negative reciprocity. A similar representation of preferences had previously been estimated by Bellemare, Kröger, and Van Soest (2008b), who capture preference heterogeneity using the parametric approach discussed above. Bruhin, Fehr, and Schunk (2019) instead allow the distribution of preferences to follow a finite mixture. Their analysis favors a mixing distribution with 3 different preference types. They also present estimates of preferences at the subject level, an approach we now discuss.

Individual-level estimation approach: Individual-level estimation amounts to estimating the model parameters separately for each subject in the sample. This can be done, for example, using the two-step approach outlined in Section 4. Using the two-step indirect approach has the added advantage of allowing estimation of a wide class of models all the while allowing the noise parameter λ to vary across subjects.

One slight complication which results from individual-level estimation is separating observable and unobservable heterogeneity. In practice, estimated individual parameters rather than true parameter values are regressed on a set of observable characteristics. For these inferences on observable characteristic to be unbiased and consistent, deviations between true and estimated preference parameters should satisfy the following assumptions: they are additive, uncorrelated with observable characteristics, and uncorrelated with the unobserved preference heterogeneity.[15] The credibility of these assumptions will depend on the model that is estimated. Consider a preference parameter θ_i restricted for theoretical reasons to the $[0, +\infty)$ interval and assume that a specific socio-demographic group (defined by given value of z_i) has $\theta_i = 0$.[16] Sampling variability and possible noise in decision-making will cause individual-level estimates $\hat{\theta}_i$ to always exceed 0. More importantly, these deviations would be correlated with z_i.

It is important to mention that researchers adopting the individual-level estimation approach will very likely need to adapt their experimental design to make sure that there are enough choices and variations in the model explanatory variables to precisely estimate model parameters for each subject. The following subsection discusses this issue in more detail.

4.3 Design of Experiments and Value Function Heterogeneity

It is of great interest to measure value function heterogeneity across the population of interest. This heterogeneity informs researchers about the nature of different decision rules used by subjects in an experiment. The behavioral economics literature has particularly focused on estimating preference heterogeneity. Identification and estimation of $f(\theta_i)$ benefits greatly from observing multiple choices for each player. Intuitively, observing the behavior of the same subject under different conditions provides information about the specific decision rules of each subject. One possibility to obtain multiple decisions per subject is to repeat a given experiment over several rounds under different conditions. Alternatively, the strategy method allows researchers to collect data on decisions of a given subject over the complete choice space. The latter

---

[15] These assumptions are those of linear regression model with a proxy dependent variable. Let θ_i denote the true preference parameter value of subject i, $\hat{\theta}_i$ the individual-level estimate, and define $v_i = \hat{\theta}_i - \theta_i$. Further, assume $\theta_i = z_i\gamma + u_i$ captures the relationship between preference parameters and observable characteristics z_i, where u_i captures the part that is unexplained by observable characteristics. Unbiased and consistent estimates of γ require that v_i is uncorrelated with both z_i and u_i. See Wooldridge (2010) for details.

[16] In the case of the Fehr and Schmidt (1999) model for example, selfish subjects have $(\alpha_i = \beta_i = 0)$.

is more appealing for specific behavioral models when some key parameters identify how subjects respond under conditions occurring less frequently. Fehr and Schmidt (1999) preferences, for example, to have a characteristic kink near payoff equalizing outcomes. Identification of aversion to having less and aversion to having more requires choice data allowing researchers to observe behavior under both scenarios. However, it may be that there are often few observed offers placing responders in a very advantageous position. A classic setting for this to occur is the ultimatum game where very advantageous offers are rarely observed. This will unlikely change by repeating the experiment over multiple rounds with (say) different proposers. Another practice is to ask respondents to state a minimal acceptable offer. One of the most striking results in Bellemare, Kröger, and Van Soest (2008a) is that a sizeable share of respondents in the ultimatum game reject disadvantageous offers, accept fair offers, but eventually reject offers that are too advantageous (termed "plateau behavior" in that paper). Asking for minimal acceptable offers would not allow to identify the incidence of such behavior. The strategy method would overcome these problems while providing researchers with multiple decisions per subject. However, the strategy method raises other issues related to the impact the elicitation method has on the decisions of subjects (see Brandts and Charness [2011] for an overview). With that said, some form of compromise about the design will in general be necessary to estimate heterogeneity of decision rules.

Neglecting using multiple decisions per subject to estimate value function heterogeneity can be hazardous. To illustrate, we conducted a simple estimation exercise on simulated data.[17] The data used for estimation simulate choices for 100 responders in an ultimatum game. In the simulation, ten possible shares of the available endowment of the proposers could be offered: $\{0, 0.1, 0.2, ..., 1\}$. We purposefully excluded offers of an share of the endowment to facilitate identification of the preferences specified below which involves a kink at payoff-equalizing offers.[18]

Preferences for each responder in the simulation were drawn from the following data-generating process:

$$\alpha_i = 0.5 + u_i^\alpha \text{ where } u_i^\alpha \sim \mathcal{N}(0, 0.5)$$
$$\beta_i = 0.3 + u_i^\beta \text{ where } u_i^\alpha \sim \mathcal{N}(0, 0.5)$$

---

[17] The online appendix contains the code (**discrete.do**) and data file (*responders.dta*) used for the simulation.

[18] This design feature was used by Bellemare, Kröger, and Van Soest (2008a), who focus on estimating nonlinear Fehr and Schmidt (1999) preferences.

$$\lambda = 0.5$$
$$Corr(u_i^\alpha, u_i^\beta) = 0.5.$$

The simulated sample contained 10 decisions for each responder, one for each of the 10 possible offers, akin to a design using the strategy method.

The data-generating process displays individual-level preference heterogeneity. Of particular interest is to compare estimates of the preference distribution for two cases. We first estimated the preference distribution using only one decision for each responder. To proceed, we randomly selected for each responder one of the 10 available offers using the following distribution: 50% chance that an offer is 0.4, 30% chance that an offer is 0.3, 10% chance that an offer is 0.2, and 10% chance that an offer is 0.6). This distribution mimics a rather common distribution of offers in the ultimatum game, with a significant share of offers close to the equal split, followed by some disadvantageous offers, and slightly fewer advantageous offers. Model estimation is then conducted using the response decision corresponding to the offer drawn for each responder.[19] Note that the correlation coefficient between α_i and β_i is not identified here given data of the same responder facing both advantageous and disadvantageous offers is not included in the estimation. Intuitively, identification of correlation at the individual level requires observing behavior of a given responder in both circumstances. Table 1 presents Conditional Logit estimates obtained using a single decision per subject using the two-step indirect approach of Section 4. We find that sample estimates diverge considerably from population values and are generally imprecisely measured. We next estimated the complete model using all available data by fitting a Mixed Logit Model using the two-step indirect approach discussed in Section 4.2. Here, the true data-generating process is estimated. Although the analysis relies on a single sample drawn from the population, we nonetheless expect to be close to population values set for the simulation. Results are presented in Table 1. As expected, we find that sample estimates are broadly in line with the corresponding population values.

Of related interest is to analyze the impact of neglecting preference heterogeneity and estimating a common value of α and β. Table 1 presents the estimates of a Conditional Logit model using all 10 decisions. By and large we find that neglecting heterogeneity leads to an increase in the estimated value of β which is now estimated to be almost twice the estimated value of α despite

---

[19] The offer that is drawn in the data file *responders.dta* is identified using the variable **hot** which takes a value of 1 for the selected offer, and 0 otherwise.

Table 1 Fehr and Schmidt (1999) model estimates using simulated data of responder decisions in an ultimatum game. Results without heterogeneity using 1 decision per subject are obtained by estimating a Conditional Logit model using the two-step indirect approach presented in Section 4. Estimates using 10 decisions per subject based on the Mixed Logit model and the two-step indirect approach presented in Section 4.2. $N = 100$

| | No heterogeneity | | With heterogeneity |
	1 decision/subject	10 decisions/subject	10 decisions/subject
α	0.591	0.323	0.382
	(0.145)	(0.065)	(0.099)
β	1.321	0.582	0.436
	(0.868)	(0.109)	(0.167)
$var(\alpha_i)$	–	–	0.442
			(0.208)
$var(\beta_i)$	–	–	0.528
			(0.283)
$corr(\alpha_i, \beta_i)$	–	–	0.575
			(0.192)
λ	0.144	0.446	0.431
	(0.034)	(0.065)	(0.064)

the fact that α is higher than β in the population. The preceding exercise underscores the importance of using multiple decisions per subject if the objective is to recover estimates of value function/preference heterogeneity.[20] At a deeper level, evidence of value function heterogeneity at the subject level is easy to find in behavioral economics. Given this, the simulation exercise suggests that it is hazardous to consider estimating a structural model using a single decision per subject given such limited information at the subject level would likely constraint researchers to impose value function homogeneity in their population, resulting in estimation of a misspecified model.

Finally, the previous subsection presented three approaches (parametric, finite-mixture, individual-level estimation) to model heterogeneity across subjects. It is often the case that statistical precision diminishes when moving from estimation of a parametric model to estimation of a nonparametric model (see e.g. Li and Racine, 2007). One can thus expect that estimating the distribution

---

[20] Estimates of the Mixed Logit model using the two-step indirect approach did not converge when estimation was based on a single randomly drawn decision per subject (**hot**=1). This is expected given correlation between α_i and β_i is not identified in this case.

of structural parameters using a finite-mixture or individual-level estimation approach would require more observations per subject and possibly more variation of the model explanatory variables at the individual level in order to obtain precise estimates. In the case of individual-level estimation for example, estimates of a nonlinear model such as the Conditional Logit will be formally consistent when the number of decisions per subject tend toward infinity. What this implies in practice is not clear except that a large number of decisions per subject are needed. Good practice would be to perform a Monte Carlo simulation exercise to determine an appropriate design before embarking in data collection and model estimation. To illustrate the importance of this point, individual-level estimation was conducted for the 100 responders in the simulated sample just discussed. In particular, a Conditional Logit model was fitted for each responder using their 10 decisions. Estimation of (α_i, β_i) failed to converge for 9 responders. For others, estimated values of α_i were never significantly different from zero at the 5% level. Moreover, almost all estimates of β_i that were significant at the 5% level took on values close to or in excess of 1, vary far from the population mean that was set for the simulation. This suggests that the design underlying the simulation is appropriate to estimate a parametric distribution of preferences but is inadequate to perform individual-level estimation.[21]

4.4 Multiplicity of Preferences

Several preference functionals have been proposed to explain behavior in field and laboratory experiments. Such functionals notably include (but are not restricted to) outcome-based preferences discussed previously (inequity aversion, equity concerns) and belief-dependent preferences discussed in the following section.

There are two approaches to deal with multiplicity of functionals. The first approach requires the assumption that decision-makers hold several functionals simultaneously, possibly varying the weight placed on each of these motivations when making their choices. This approach amounts to adding control variables to the value function in order to capture these additional functionals. In the example above, measures of inequity to own/others disadvantages (such as those of Fehr and Schmidt [1999] above) could be added alongside guilt or belief-dependent reciprocity control variables. The challenge with this approach is insuring that the experimental design can separately identify

---

[21] The Stata file discrete.do provides the code to conduct individual-level estimation on the sample discussed here.

the different motives. Engelmann and Strobel (2004) estimate a random utility model to separate inequity aversion (Fehr and Schmidt, 1999; Bolton and Ockenfels, 2000), Maxmin preferences, and efficiency concerns. A conceptual issue with this approach is the behavioral plausibility that subjects in a given decision setting are endowed with a multiplicity of competing motivations that they balance to make a choice. The second approach is based on the assumption that the population of subjects is composed of different "types," each characterized by a single dominant functional. The empirical challenge is to recover the distribution of types using the data. This leads to a finite mixture of types, where type differ with respect to the structure of their preferences as opposed to heterogeneity of parameters of a given preference functional.

5 Uncertainty in Structural Models

The analysis of decision-making under uncertainty plays a central role in experimental and behavioral economics. So far we have primarily covered models where such uncertainty was absent (a notable exception was the principal-agent model of worker productivity in Section 2). In this section we present and discuss issues related to estimation of structural models when subjects face either uncertainty. It is important to note that estimation of most of the models presented in this section will require some programming primarily because value functions are rarely expressed as linear combinations of explanatory variables. We begin the presentation with choice situations where subjects face objective risks, or probabilities. We then consider the case where subjects face unknown probabilities. There, we will begin by covering standard econometric models where subjects are assumed to hold a unique well-defined subjective probability distribution over events. We will conclude by considering models of decision-making under ambiguity where subjects are no longer assumed to hold a unique well-defined subjective probability distribution over events. The section will also discuss various issues related to the measurement of beliefs as well as simple approaches to deal with potential endogeneity of stated beliefs.

5.1 Structural Models with Known Probabilities

There has been a large and important literature focused on measuring risk preferences using experimental designs that vary risk and/or payoff outcomes. For these endeavors, structural models have been particularly useful. A well-known example is provided by Holt and Laury (2002), who present subjects with a menu of 10 binary choices between lottery pairs. In this design, possible outcomes of lottery pairs are held constant across the 10 binary decisions while the objective probabilities associated with these outcomes vary across lottery pairs, imposing subjects with varying degrees of risk. This variation allows researchers to identify risk preference intervals depending on the choice sequence of each subject. Many other experimental designs exploit binary choices between lottery pairs (Bruhin, Fehr-Duda, and Epper, 2010; Von Gaudecker, Van Soest, and Wengstrom, 2011) to measure risk preferences.

To set ideas consider the choice between binary lottery A and binary lottery B. Furthermore, let p_A p_B be the known risks placed on the high payoff outcomes (x_h^A and x_h^B) of lotteries A and B respectively (low payoff outcomes are denoted x_l^A and x_l^B. Let $U(\cdot; \theta)$ capture the utility of subject i given the vector of preference parameters θ, and $EU_{ij}(\theta_i)$ denote expected utility of alternative j. A simple model assumes lottery A is preferred to lottery B if the expected utility of A (denoted $EU_{iA}(\theta)$) is greater than the expected utility of B (denoted $EU_{iB}(\theta)$), that is

$$\overbrace{p_A U(x_h^A; \theta) + (1 - p_A)U(x_l^A; \theta)}^{EU_{iA}(\theta)} > \overbrace{p_B U(x_h^B; \theta) + (1 - p_B)U(x_l^B; \theta)}^{EU_{iB}(\theta)}. \qquad (27)$$

The shape of the utility function (increasing convex, linear, concave) captures the risk preferences of subject i. Different parametrizations of $U(\cdot; \theta)$ have been used in the empirical literature (see Holt and Laury [2014] for an overview). Two very popular parametric functionals for $U(\cdot; \theta_i)$ are the power utility function capturing constant relative risk aversion (CRRA), and the exponential utility function capturing constant absolute risk aversion (CARA). In both cases, $\theta = \theta$, a scalar parameter.[22]

Again, randomness needs to be accounted for to bring this model to data. A natural way of introducing randomness is to revert to one of the approaches discussed in the previous sections, namely either incorporating in the model preference heterogeneity, random disturbances, or a hybrid of both approaches. Many experiments were designed to capture risk preference heterogeneity, and results from these experiments overwhelmingly support the existence of such heterogeneity. As a result, neglecting this apparent feature of almost any subject population is questionable. This explains why many structural models in this area recover estimates of risk preferences using a hybrid approach by estimating models with both preference heterogeneity and random disturbances/noise in decision-making.

Following our previous notation, a RUM approach leads to a specification of value functions (here capturing expected utility) measured with error that have the following additive structure:

---

[22] An example of a nonscalar parametrization of utility is the power-expo function used in Holt and Laury (2002).

$$\tilde{V}_{ij}(\boldsymbol{\theta}_i) = V_{ij}(\boldsymbol{\theta}_i) + \lambda \epsilon_{ij}$$
$$= EU_{ij}(\boldsymbol{\theta}) + \lambda \epsilon_{ij}, \tag{28}$$

where $j = \{A, B\}$ indexes the lottery and ϵ_{ij} have been defined in Section 4.1. There are two issues that require discussion that apply specifically to structural estimation of risk preferences. First, the scale of value functions $V_{ij}(\boldsymbol{\theta})$ is a function of the utility function $U(\cdot; \boldsymbol{\theta})$ itself and thus varies with the shape of their respective functions (different values of $\boldsymbol{\theta}$). This feature complicates interpretation of λ given the signal-to-noise ratio (differences in V_{ij}) to that of noise ϵ_{it} is affected by the individual utility function parameters. As Von Gaudecker, Van Soest, and Wengstrom (2011) argue, value functions computed on the basis of certainty equivalents of each lottery facilitate interpretation of the noise signal and comparisons across subjects. This follows because certainty equivalents measure the value of an alternative in monetary terms, given the risk preferences of subjects.[23] This leads to the following modified value function

$$V_{ij}(\boldsymbol{\theta}) + \lambda \epsilon_{ij} = CE_{ij}(\boldsymbol{\theta}) + \lambda \epsilon_{ij}, \tag{29}$$

where $CE_{ij}(\boldsymbol{\theta})$ denotes the certainty equivalent of subject i for lottery j given their risk preference parameter values.[24] This approach effectively uses a monetary scale to compare lotteries at the subject level. Also, working with certainty equivalents also means that λ can separately be estimated without imposing other normalizations on the utility function.[25] Von Gaudecker, Van Soest, and Wengstrom (2011) adopt a hybrid approach and estimate risk preferences using a random utility model with preference heterogeneity (see Section 4.2). In their model, value functions (V_{ij}) are evaluated using certainty equivalents to which random disturbances are added. Their model additionally features loss aversion and preference for early/late resolution of uncertainty (see Kreps and Porteus, 1978). They estimate their model using a random sample of 1422 Dutch respondents participating in an online panel (LISS panel). All parameters of their model (risk, loss, uncertainty resolution, noise) are allowed to vary across a rich set of observable socio-economic characteristics. They also capture unobserved heterogeneity across all model parameters. They notably find that unobserved heterogeneity explains the bulk of the measured heterogeneity in preferences and noise in their population.

---

[23] Certainty equivalents represent the fixed monetary value that would make a subject indifferent between accepting it or opting for a specific risky alternative/lottery.

[24] Explicit expressions for $CE_{ij}(\boldsymbol{\theta})$ exist for CARA, CRRA, and other related utility functions; see Von Gaudecker, Van Soest, and Wengstrom (2011) for details.

[25] Conte, Hey, and Moffatt (2011), for example, model risk-taking behavior using a structure similar to (28) but normalize utility to the unit interval which allows them to separately estimate the noise parameter.

It should be noted that other approaches have been used to capture noise in risky choice experiments. One such alternative (see Holt and Laury, 2002; Andersen et al., 2008) is based on the work of Luce (1959). The probability of choosing lottery A over lottery B in the binary choice case is given by

$$\Pr(Choose = A) = \frac{EU_{iA}(\theta)^{1/\mu}}{EU_{iA}(\theta)^{1/\mu} + EU_{iB}(\theta)^{1/\mu}}, \tag{30}$$

where μ is a noise parameter. In this specification, the probability of choosing A over B converges to 0.5 as the noise parameter μ increases in value. A subject facing such high noise levels is in effect tossing a coin to choose between both lotteries. On the other hand, the probability of choosing the lottery maximizing expected utility approaches 1 as μ tends toward 0.

Assessing the preferred way to capture risk-taking behavior requires comparing specifications using a common metric, as, for example, via a goodness-of-fit analysis, both within and out-of-sample. This issue is discussed later in Section 6. Also. all RUM models above can be extended to allow for preference heterogeneity of θ using the approaches discussed in Section 4.2. Von Gaudecker, Van Soest, and Wengstrom (2011) and Wilcox (2011), for example, model the distribution of risk preferences using parametric distributional assumptions. Bruhin, Fehr-Duda, and Epper (2010) estimate the distribution of risk preferences using a finite mixture approach. Conte, Hey, and Moffatt (2011) use a hybrid approach: they model their population as a finite mixture of two types (expected utility and rand-dependent expected utility). They also specify and parametric distributions of risk preferences within each type. Hey and Orme (1994) perform individual-level estimation for various models of risk-taking behavior.

Apesteguia and Ballester (2018) recently discussed identification problems associated with estimation of risk preferences based on random utility models. Consider the choice between lottery A or B discussed above. We follow Apesteguia and Ballester (2018) and illustrate the identification problem using the following numeral parametrization. Let lottery A be a risky lottery paying $1 with probability 0.9, and $60 with probability 0.1. Furthermore, let lottery B be a degenerate lottery paying $5 with certainty. Furthermore, add type 1 extreme value random disturbances to the expected utility of both lotteries, as in (28).

It follows that the probability of choosing the risky lottery A is given by

$$\Pr(Choose = A) = \frac{\exp(EU_{iA}(\theta)/\lambda)}{\exp(EU_{iA}(\theta)/\lambda) + \exp(EU_{iB}(\theta)/\lambda)}. \tag{31}$$

One would expect the probability of choosing the risky lottery A to be monotonically decreasing with risk aversion θ, ultimately tending toward zero

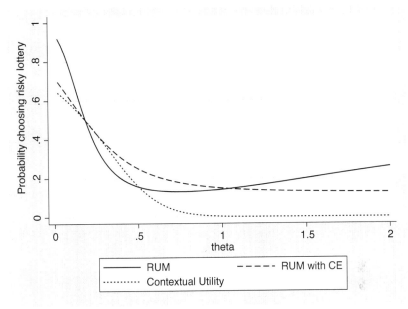

Figure 1 Predicted probability of choosing risky lottery A as a function of the risk aversion parameter θ for the basis random utility model (RUM), the random utility model using certainty equivalents (RUM with CE), and the random utility model with contextual utility (contextual utility). Utility function is given by $U(x; \theta) = \frac{x^{1-\theta}}{1-\theta}$. Noise parameter λ set to 0.66, 2, and 0.005 for RUM, RUM with CE, and contextual utility respectively.

for very risk-averse subjects. However, this is not always the case. Figure 1 plots the probability of choosing the risky lottery A as a function of the risk aversion parameter θ, setting $\lambda = 2/3$ and such that the utility function is given by $U(x; \theta) = \frac{x^{1-\theta}}{1-\theta}$. We see that the probability of choosing the risky lottery initially decreases with risk aversion before increasing back again for very high levels of risk aversion. This nonmonotone relationship is problematic as it implies that possibly two levels of risk aversion are consistent with low proportions of risky lottery choices. This nonmonotone relationship is related to the scale of utility which varies with the level of risk aversion. In particular, the cardinal value of the difference in expected utility between both lotteries $(EU_{i,A}(\theta) - EU_{i,B}(\theta))$ diminishes (becomes flat) when θ increases. For a given level of noise λ, this decrease implies that the noise level eventually dominates differences in value functions across alternatives, translating in an increasing probability of incorrectly opting for the risky lottery for very risk-averse subjects.

It is clear that imposing a constant level of noise λ for all levels of risk aversion drives the non-monotonicity described above. This was noted by

Wilcox (2011), who proposes a RUM approach called "contextual utility" which re-scales valuations of lotteries ($EU_{ij}(\boldsymbol{\theta})$ in (31)) by dividing them with the difference between the maximal and minimal utilities $U(.; \boldsymbol{\theta})$ over outcomes x_o^j across all lotteries j in the choice set (where o indexes outcomes for lottery j). Wilcox (2011) applies this normalization to the analysis of choice between pairs of lotteries each involving three possible outcomes. Consider instead the use of certainty equivalents discussed above:

$$\Pr(Choose = A) = \frac{\exp(CE_{iA}(\theta)/\lambda)}{\exp(CE_{iA}(\theta)/\lambda) + \exp(CE_{iB}(\theta)/\lambda)}. \tag{32}$$

Intuitively, increasing θ does not alter the scale of differences of certainty equivalents relative to the noise level λ. Put differently, the valuation of lotteries using certainty equivalents uses a common metric for all subjects regardless of the level of θ.

Figure 1 plots the corresponding predicted choice probability for the previous numerical example using certainty equivalents (equation (32) setting $\lambda = 2$) and the contextual utility model of Wilcox (2011) (setting $\lambda = 0.05$)). We find that using certainty equivalents or the contextual utility model restores monotonicity in this numerical example. Unfortunately, this is not a general result. Apesteguia and Ballester (2018) show that the monotonicity achieved using certainty equivalents in Figure 1 arises because one of the two lotteries is degenerate. This follows because the certainty equivalent of lottery A decreases with θ while that of lottery B (a degenerate lottery) is held constant. As a result, the difference in certainty equivalents between both lotteries will monotonically decrease with θ for a given value of λ, explaining Figure 1. They show (see their Corollary 2) that nonmonotonicity may emerge in other lottery choice pairings even when using certainty equivalents. Similarly, they provide (see p. 97 of their paper) a lottery choice example where the contextual utility model of Wilcox (2011) violates monotonicity.[26] More generally, Apesteguia and Ballester (2018) prove that RUM approaches (not just the logit RUM in the numerical example above) violates monotonicity in settings where subjects are asked to compare pairs of nondegenerate lotteries where one is riskier than the other. They also show that increasing lottery payoffs exacerbates the problem.

Apesteguia and Ballester (2018) introduce the random parameter model (RPM) as an alternative to the RUM approach. They show that the RPM preserves monotonicity and thus overcomes the identification problem discussed above. In the RPM, randomness is introduced only through unobserved heterogeneity of the risk preferences of subjects. In particular, this model

---

[26] In this example, subjects are faced with a choice between two lotteries, each with five possible outcomes, where one lottery is a mean-preserving spread of the other.

$$U(x_{ij}; \theta_i) = U(x_{ij}; \theta + \epsilon_i), \tag{33}$$

where ϵ_i follows a monotone cumulative distribution function over the space of risk preferences. The model is estimated by Maximum Likelihood, where the choice probabilities are derived using the assumed distribution for ϵ_i. The choice probability in the special case where ϵ_i is specified to follow a logistic distribution has the following simple form:

$$\Pr(Choose = A) = \frac{\exp(\overline{\theta}/\lambda)}{\exp(\overline{\theta}/\lambda) + \exp(\theta/\lambda)}, \tag{34}$$

where $\overline{\theta}$ denotes the indifference level of risk aversion θ_i such that $EU_{iA}(\overline{\theta}) = EU_{iB}(\overline{\theta})$. Inspection of (34) reveals that increasing θ increases the value of the denominator in the equation, thus monotonically decreasing the probability of choosing the risky lottery A.[27] Apesteguia and Ballester (2018) revisit estimation of risk preferences using data from Andersen et al. (2008). They find that the estimated level of risk aversion is 14% higher when estimated using the monotonicity preserving RPM model relative to estimates from a RUM. Moreover, concordant with their theoretical analysis, bias of estimated population levels of risk aversion were found to increase when estimation was restricted to more risk-averse subjects. Applications of the random parameter model approach to estimate risk aversion includes Barsky et al. (1997) and Kimball, Sahm, and Shapiro (2008).[28]

The preceding discussion highlights the value of clearly defining the objectives of a structural model before implementing a design and conducting experiments. A discussed above, there are experimental designs where all approaches are expected to solve the nonmonotonicity problem (certainty equivalents, contextual utility model, random parameter model of Apesteguia and Ballester [2018]), and designs where only the approach of Apesteguia and Ballester (2018) solves the problem. If the objective is to recover risk preferences in more general choice settings, then this should steer researchers away from RUM approaches and toward a RPM approach. With that said, implementing the RPM approach is simple when risk preferences are assumed governed by a single parameter (such as in CRRA or CARA). With more than one random parameter (for example the power-expo utility function used in Holt and Laury [2002]), implementation of the RPM is more tricky a researchers need to

---

[27] Given $\overline{\theta}$, the probability of choosing lottery A is given by $\Pr(\theta + \epsilon_i \leq \overline{\theta}) = \Phi(\overline{\theta} - \theta)$, where $\Phi(\cdot)$ is the cumulative distribution function of ϵ_i that is assumed.

[28] Some researchers advocate using an interval regression approach to estimate the distribution of risk aversion (see e.g. Wik et al., 2004). It is important to note that this approach coincides with the random parameter approach described here.

compute the probability that the (now) vector $\boldsymbol{\theta}_i$ falls in the region where a given subject who prefer a given lottery over the other. This computation requires first solving for the frontier in the space of $\boldsymbol{\theta}_i$ where subjects are indifferent between lotteries.

Nonlinear Probability Weighting

There is a vast literature on nonlinear probability weighting in choice experiments with known risks (see Wakker [2010] for an overview). Expanding on the previous example, subjects will choose Lottery A over Lottery B when

$$w_i(p_A)U(x_h^A;\boldsymbol{\theta})+w_i((1-p_A))U(x_l^A;\boldsymbol{\theta}) > w_i(p_B)U(x_h^B;\boldsymbol{\theta})+w_i((1-p_B))U(x_l^B;\boldsymbol{\theta}),$$

(35)

where $w_i(\cdot)$ denotes the probability weighting function of subject i. One popular specification (see Goldstein and Einhorn, 1987) is

$$w_i(p_j) = \frac{\delta_i p_j^{\gamma_i}}{\delta_i p_j^{\gamma_i} + (1-p_j)^{\gamma_i}},$$

(36)

where ($\delta_i \geq 0, \gamma_i \geq 0$) are parameters to be estimated alongside $\boldsymbol{\theta}_i$. Expected Utility ((27)) is typically a special case (with ($\delta_i = 1, \gamma_i = 1$) in (36) above).[29] Hey and Orme (1994) estimate a variety of structural models using lottery choice data from 80 subjects each making 100 choices between lottery pairs. One of the models they estimate uses the weighting function proposed by Quiggin (1982) which is a special case of 36 setting $\delta_i = 1$. The high number of choices per subject allows estimation of each model at the individual level. All their models are estimated using a RUM approach with normally distributed errors. In stark contrast, Camerer and Ho (1994) also estimate the weighting function proposed by Quiggin (1982) using a RUM approach but do not allow for heterogeneity across subjects (a common value of γ_i is estimated), owing to the fact they do not have many decisions per subject. More recently, Bruhin, Fehr-Duda, and Epper (2010) and Conte, Hey, and Moffatt (2011) both classify subjects according to their risk preferences and probability weighting using finite mixture models. As discussed previously, Conte, Hey, and Moffatt (2011) model risk-taking behavior using (28), normalizing utility accordingly. Bruhin, Fehr-Duda, and Epper (2010) model risk-taking behavior using certainty equivalents of respective lotteries and add a random disturbance as in (29). Certainty equivalents are defined on basis of a power utility function and probability weighting captured using the following specification of Goldstein and Einhorn

---

[29] See Wakker (2010) for other popular weighting functions used in the literature.

(1987). They estimate their model using data from a sequence of 20 pairwise choices of binary lotteries.

Conte, Hey, and Moffatt (2011) estimate a selection of structural models using experimental data from a risk-taking experiment. Models vary the utility function (CARA and CRRA) as well as the weighting function distorting outcome probabilities. They notably consider the Quiggin (1982) weighting function which is closely related to (36) as well as a power-weighting function. Their treatment of parameter heterogeneity differs from Bruhin, Fehr-Duda, and Epper (2010). In particular, they assume the population comprises a finite mixture of two preference types: Expected Utility and Rank-dependent Expected Utility maximizers. In contrast, Bruhin, Fehr-Duda, and Epper (2010) do not impose ex ante that expected utility maximizers are one of the types of the mixture they estimate. Both studies model heterogeneity in preferences and weighting by specifying a finite mixture distribution of the model parameters. Furthermore, both studies find that a large share of subjects use nonlinear probability weighting, violating expected utility theory.

It should be said that allowing for nonlinear probability weighting does not solve the issues raised by Apesteguia and Ballester (2018) and discussed above regarding a potential identification problem associated with estimation based on the RUM approach. Also, the literature on nonlinear probability weighting has considered parameter free approaches to measure both utility and nonlinear weighting functions (see e.g. Abdellaoui, 2000). These approaches can be used to generate estimates under weaker assumptions than those imposed by the parametric structural models surveyed above.

5.2 Structural Models with Subjective Probabilities

In this section we discuss structural models when subjects using subjective beliefs/expectations. We present models according to the source of uncertainty. Models with uncertainty about the actions of others are discussed first. Models with uncertainty about the beliefs of others follow.

Uncertainty about Actions and Payoffs

Structural models for decision-making under uncertainty typically combine two behavioral components – beliefs/expectations and preferences. This feature raises new identification issues given each component should be separately identified and estimated. Manski (2002) argues that many sets of preferences and beliefs can be consistent with the same choice data in popular economic experiments of proposal and response (ultimatum and trust games). This identification problem is more general in nature and has direct implications for inferences on preferences when subjects face uncertainty, as estimated preferences will tend adjust to the assumptions maintained about the beliefs of subjects in order to fit the data.

Identification without Stated Belief Data

One way to solve this identification problem is to fix beliefs of subjects to some measurable quantity, for example assuming subjects hold rational expectations. Under this assumption, beliefs can be separately estimated using the observed choices in the experiment. An example of this is given in Bruyn and Bolton (2008), who estimate a version of the model of outcome-based preferences of Bolton and Ockenfels (2000) (see (21)) using data from ultimatum game experiments. They obtain preference estimates under the assumption that proposers have rational expectations. The plausibility of this approach is questionable, especially in experimental settings where subjects have limited prior experience with both the game and limited knowledge about the subject pool they interact with. A very different approach is to try to estimate both beliefs and preferences from the choice data alone. Conte et al. (2012) estimates both risk preferences and beliefs using Italian games how data. There, the authors exploit choice data from the final round of the games how where subjects' beliefs are irrelevant. Decisions in these final rounds thus identify preferences. Conditional on the preferences, beliefs in earlier rounds are identified under additional assumptions, including homogeneity of beliefs across subjects and independence of beliefs and risk preferences. There are reasons to believe these are restrictive assumptions. In particular, homogeneity of subjective beliefs will almost surely be rejected when belief data are collected. Also, some studies have found significant correlations between subjective beliefs and preferences in other domains (e.g. Bellemare, Kröger, and Van Soest, 2008a).

Another related approach to separately identify the effects of beliefs and preferences combines data from related games. Cox (2004), for example, proposes a design to identify trust, reciprocity, and other-regarding preferences. In this design, a subset of subjects play the investment game of Berg, Dickhaut, and McCabe (1995). There, "senders" decide how much of an endowment to transfer to "receivers," while the latter decide how much to transfer back to senders. Hence, the decision of senders combines their beliefs (trust) about the amount receivers will return to them with their preferences about final allocations for both players. Cox (2004) separates the role of beliefs (the trust component) from preferences by comparing behavior in that game with behavior in a related treatment where senders are placed in the role of dictators who determine the final allocation of both players. Dictators face no uncertainty, and thus there is no trust component, with their decisions driven solely by their preferences about final allocations.[30] Again, separate identification of the effects of beliefs and preferences requires the assumption that preferences are similar across the various decision tasks. While subjects (and thus the set of preference distributions) may indeed be randomized across decisions and games, the role and games themselves may trigger the use of specific preferences within the set.[31]

Identification Using Stated Belief Data

A more promising approach is to elicit beliefs and combine the latter with choice data to estimate preferences, taking into account randomness and noise in both choices and stated belief/expectations data. An example of this is given in Bellemare, Kröger, and Van Soest (2008a), who focus on estimating the distribution of inequity aversion in a large and representative sample of the Dutch population using proposer and responder decisions in an ultimatum game. Proposers in their experiment could offer one of 10 possible shares of a fixed endowment. Responders played the strategy method, providing acceptance/rejection decisions conditional on each of the 10 offers occurring.

They consider two models based on Fehr and Schmidt (1999) preferences. Both models differ with respect to the assumptions maintained about the uncertainty faced by proposers in the experiment. The first model assumes that proposers maximize subjective expected utility. In particular, let Q_{ij} denote subject i's subjective probability that offer j will be accepted by the responder. The value of offer $j \in \{1, 2, ..., 10\}$ if accepted was modeled using the following value function:

$$
\begin{aligned}
V_{ij} &= Q_{ij}(\pi_{ia} - \alpha_{1i} \max(0, \Pi - 2\pi_{ia}) - \beta_{1i} \max(0, 2\pi_{ia} - \Pi) \\
&\quad - \alpha_2 \max(0, \Pi - 2\pi_{ia})^2 - \beta_2 \max(0, 2\pi_{ia} - \Pi)^2) \\
&= \mathbf{x}_{ij}\theta,
\end{aligned}
\tag{37}
$$

where

$$
\mathbf{x}_{ij} = Q_{ij}\left[\pi_{ij}, \max(0, \Pi - 2\pi_{ia}), \max(0, 2\pi_{ia} - \Pi), \right.
$$
$$
\left. \max(0, \Pi - 2\pi_{ia})^2, \max(0, 2\pi_{ia} - \Pi)^2\right]
$$
$$
\theta = (1, -\alpha_1, -\beta_1, -\alpha_2, -\beta_2)'.
$$

---

[30] Cox (2004) additionally implements a third treatment to separately identify whether transfers made by receivers in the investment game are driven by reciprocal preferences or distributional concerns about the final allocation.

[31] For example, Bellemare, Kröger, and Van Soest (2008a) find that inequity aversion differs significantly between proposers and responders in the ultimatum game.

Nonlinear inequity aversion was captured by the additional explanatory variables $(\max(0, \Pi - 2\pi_{ia}))^2$ and $(\max(0, 2\pi_{ia} - \Pi))^2$. Furthermore, observed and unobserved heterogeneity were modeled using the parametric approach (see Section 4.2). They notably specified $(\alpha_{1i}, \beta_{1i})$ to be jointly log-normally distributed, where the (log) average parameters were allowed to depend on a set of observable characteristics of panel subjects. This model can thus be estimated using the two-step indirect approach outlined previously, constructing all variables entering $\mathbf{x}_{ij}$ given observed payoffs and elicited beliefs Q_{ij}.[32]

The second model considered by Bellemare, Kröger, and Van Soest (2008a) assumed that proposers have rational expectations. This was implemented by replacing Q_{ij} by the corresponding observed average acceptance rates of responders for each of the 10 possible offers. Responder behavior was modeled using similar preferences, and both models (subjective and rational expectations) were estimated combining data of proposers and responders.[33]

The analysis above assumes that each subject is able to form a unique well-defined subjective probability distribution over the different possible states of the world and is also able to compute subjective valuations of each alternative in their choice set. Starting with Ellsberg (1961), there has been a large body of evidence questioning the capacity of individuals to form and act on such precise probability distributions. Models of decision-making under ambiguity instead focus on settings where subjects do not make decisions on the basis of a single probability distribution over the different states of the world. Two of the most popular models of decision-making under ambiguity are the Maxmin expected utility model (MEU) of Gilboa and Schmeidler (1989) and the smooth ambiguity model of Klibanoff, Marinacci, and Mukerji (2005) (see Wakker [2010] for a detailed discussion of these and other models of decision-making under ambiguity). Both models assume decision-makers hold a set rather than a unique

---

[32] The model using subjective probabilistic data estimated in Bellemare, Kröger, and Van Soest (2008a) additionally controlled for possible measurement errors and biases due to framing (acceptance/rejection) of the elicited probabilities, denoted P_{ij}. This allowed the elicited probabilities P_{ij} to differ from the true unobserved subjective probabilities Q_{ij}.

[33] Value functions for responders were given by:

$$V_{ia} = \pi_{ia} - \alpha_1 \max(0, \Pi - 2\pi_{ia}) - \beta_1 \max(0, 2\pi_{ia} - \Pi)$$
$$- \alpha_2 \max(0, \Pi - 2\pi_{ia})^2 - \beta_2 \max(0, 2\pi_{ia} - \Pi)^2$$
$$= \mathbf{x}_{ia}\theta$$

such that $\mathbf{x}_{ia}$ contains all explanatory variables and

$$\theta = (1, -\alpha_1, -\beta_1, -\alpha_2, -\beta_2)'.$$

Role-specific preferences were captured by allowing α_1 and β_1 to vary between proposers and responders.

probability distribution over states of the world. The MEU model assumes that decision-makers compute the minimum possible expected utility of each alternative before selecting the alternative maximizing these minimal expected utility values. MEU decision-makers are thus modeled as pessimistic evaluators of the worst-case scenario for each alternative.[34] The smooth ambiguity model assumes decision-makers are able to place a subjective weight (a second-order probability) on the possible probabilities distributions in their set. As such, decision-makers potentially consider all possible distributions, not just those yielding extreme expected utilities. One of the main advantages of the smooth ambiguity model over MEU is that perceived ambiguity (beliefs) and ambiguity attitudes/preferences (averse, neutral, seeking) are clearly separated. This offers a clear advantage from a modeling perspective given the smooth ambiguity model offers the possibility to model both how agents update their perceived ambiguity and their ambiguity attitudes/preferences. Various experimental tests of both models have been conducted (Baillon and Bleichrodt, 2015; Cubitt, Van De Kuilen, and Mukerji, 2020). The evidence from these tests is mixed and suggests that findings may depend on the choice of experimental design and experimental methods.

Contrary to the analysis of risk in Section 5.1, models of ambiguity incorporate a subjective component which requires measurement before estimating a structural model. In particular, the set of possible distributions as well as the weights placed on the distributions themselves (in the case of the smooth model of ambiguity) should in principle be elicited. These are challenging endeavors which may explain the relative scarcity of structural work in this area. In fact, existing structural work on models with ambiguity makes some compromise in terms of design in order to make estimation feasible. Conte and Hey (2013), for example, provide individual-estimates as well as estimates of a finite mixture of preference types using an experimental design involving compound lotteries. The preference types considered include expected utility, the smooth ambiguity model, rank-dependent utility, and α-MEU. They find that close to 50% of subjects behave according to the smooth ambiguity model, with 25% behaving according to expected utility theory.[35] Here, the use of objective compound lotteries avoids the need to elicit ambiguity from subjects. However, doing so introduces a clear gap between structural model estimates which thus capture attitudes toward compound risks and the underlying theoretical models of

---

[34] Variations of MEU include the α-MEU model (Hurwicz, 1951).

[35] Other experimental papers comparing models of decision-making under ambiguity include Hey, Lotito, and Maffioletti (2010) and Kothiyal, Spinu, and Wakker (2014). The analysis in these papers does not, however, consider the smooth model of ambiguity, complicating comparisons of results across papers.

ambiguity which involve a subjective component which is not present in the experiment.

Ahn et al. (2014) conduct a portfolio choice experiment. Subjects were asked to construct portfolios with three possible states of the world. The risk of one state is known (1/3) while the individual risks of the other two states are unknown – subjects only know that the combine risks of both states sums to 2/3. Subjects were not informed about the probability that the latter two states will occur, thus casting their design and analysis as ambiguity rather than compound risks. With that said, a version of the smooth model of ambiguity is estimated assuming all subjects correctly guessed the probability of each of the remaining two states would be randomly drawn from a uniform distribution. Again, this assumption is necessary given the absence of data on subjective distributions at the subject level. Estimation of all models is conducted using nonlinear least squares in combination with the first-order condition approach of Section 3. Doing so allows researchers to lessen the distributional requirements of the model relative to Maximum Likelihood estimation. They find that close to 60% of subjects behave according to subjective expected utility, with the remaining share of subjects exhibiting ambiguity aversion/seeking behavior and/or pessimism/optimism. Recently, Bellemare, Kröger, and Sossou (2020) used a novel experimental design that exogenously determines the set of possible distributions for the return of an asset. Subjects in the experiment progressively observed draws from the true return distribution over multiple periods, thus allowing them to learn which of the possible distribution is generating returns. Subjects were asked to make portfolio choices at regular intervals. Importantly, they are also asked to state and revise their subjective probability that returns are generating from each possible distribution presented. The experiment was setup with structural estimation of an extended version of the smooth model of ambiguity in mind. The model involved a rich set of preference domains (ambiguity aversion, risk aversion, and loss aversion). The distribution of these preferences is estimated both at the individual level and using a finite mixture specification with seven types. Estimation of the distribution of preferences is conducted using a random utility approach based on certainty equivalents (see Section 4.2). Updating of the stated subjectively probability assigned to each possible distribution generating returns is modeled using a generalized Bayes rule. Results suggest that ambiguity aversion dominates loss aversion as a driver of portfolio choices in the experiment, and subjects are slow to update their belies about the true distribution, thus prolonging the effects of ambiguity.

These papers highlight the progress made in structural estimation of models of decision-making under ambiguity. One can question the extent to which these papers really inform about decision-making under ambiguity when some of the core subjective elements of the underlying structural models differ from the theory. These differences underscore the need for better designs and data in order to bring theoretical and empirical models closer together.

Uncertainty about the Beliefs of Others

Battigalli and Dufwenberg (2020) provide a recent overview of belief-dependent preferences which can be modeled using the tools of psychological game theory. Preferences are typically defined over the beliefs players have about the beliefs of others. These preferences can be used to capture image concerns, reciprocity, and emotions (for example guilt aversion). We consider in more detail below the examples of belief-dependent reciprocity and guilt aversion, two of the earliest and most popular applications of psychological game theory in economics. In both cases, a psychological payoff is introduced to capture deviations from selfish behavior. Rabin (1993) was among the first to use psychological game theory to model fairness and reciprocity in economic decision-making. In his model, psychological payoff functions involved higher-order beliefs of relevant decision-makers, where beliefs and expectations were defined over the material payoffs of the game. Note that the specification of the psychological payoff function added in (5) in the motivating example of this article is inspired by Rabin (1993) yet does not involve beliefs given these were unobserved in the field experiment.

Guilt aversion and reciprocity will be illustrated using the two-player binary trust game two player binary trust game in Figure 2 used from Bellemare and Sebald (2022).

In this game, player A can either select the outside option R which effectively ends the game and provides player A and player B with material payoffs of 45 and 30, respectively. Alternatively, player A can select to play L and let player B decide the final material payoffs by selecting either l or r. The selfish option for player B is then to select l and earn 210 while providing player A with a payoff of 30. Selecting r, on the other hand, is costly for Player B as it leads to a reduction in payoff from 210 to 150. However, this option raises the material payoff of player A as long as $z > 30$. Guilt aversion and reciprocity can both explain deviations from selfish behavior for B players in this game.

Guilt aversion. Battigalli and Dufwenberg (2007) introduce models to capture emotions of guilt aversion. One of their models, coined "simple guilt," focuses on subjects suffering disutility when letting down others. In the game above, Player B may experience guilt by choosing the selfish alternative l if he believes player A expects a higher material payoff. Player B does not, however, know the material payoff expected by Player A at this stage in the game. Player B is able to make a choice after forming own expectations about the material payoff

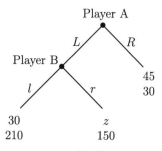

Figure 2 Binary trust games (Bellemare and Sebald (2022)).

expected by Player A, so-called higher-order beliefs. The choice faced by Player B can be modeled using the discrete choice framework of Section 4. Let $\mathbf{E}_i^A\left(\pi_i^A\right)$ denote the expected material payoff of Player A who is matched to subject i in the role of Player B, conditional on playing L. Also, let $\mathbf{E}_i^B\left(\mathbf{E}_i^A\left(\pi_i^A\right)\right)$ denote the higher-order expectations of subject i in the role of player B regarding the expected payoff of player A. It is assumed that subject i will experience guilt by choosing j if the final payoff π_{ij}^A to player A falls below $\mathbf{E}_i^B\left(\mathbf{E}_i^A\left(\pi_i^A\right)\right)$. The psychological payoff function of Player B is then given by $\max\{\mathbf{E}_i^B\left(\mathbf{E}_i^A\left(\pi_i^A\right)\right)-\pi_{ij}^A,0\}$. The latter is added to the following value function:

$$V_{ij}=\pi_{ij}^B-\phi_i\max\{\mathbf{E}_i^B\left(\mathbf{E}_i^A\left(\pi_i^A\right)\right)-\pi_{ij}^A,0\} \tag{38}$$
$$=\mathbf{x}_{ij}\boldsymbol{\theta}_i,$$

where

$$\mathbf{x}_{ij}=\left[\pi_j^B,\max\{\mathbf{E}_i^B\left(\mathbf{E}_i^A\left(\pi_i^A\right)\right)-\pi_{ij}^A,0\}\right]$$
$$\boldsymbol{\theta}_i=(1,-\phi_i)'.$$

Notice here that guilt sensitivity $\phi_i\geq0$ can vary across subjects, with higher values capturing stronger guilt aversion. Variables in $\mathbf{x}_{ij}$ can be constructed for each subject given their stated higher-order beliefs $\mathbf{E}_i^B\left(\mathbf{E}_i^A\left(\pi_i^A\right)\right)$. Estimation can then proceed using the two-step indirect approach outlined in Section 4.2, assuming, for example, a parametric distribution for ϕ_i. It is important to reiterate that multiple decisions per subject would be helpful to identify the distribution of guilt sensitivities.[36]

---

[36] Bellemare, Sebald, and Suetens (2018) estimate such a distribution for different payoff levels using data from a within-subject design experiment based on a binary dictator game. They maintain the assumption that ϕ_i follows a normal distribution where the mean of this distribution can shift across payoff levels in the experiment.

Mixed Logit with guilt aversion preferences - Stata example
(guiltaversion.do)

```
cmxtmixlogit y own, random(guilt) noconstant
nlcom lambda: 1/_b[own]
nlcom mean_alpha: _b[guilt]/_b[own]
nlcom var_alpha: _b[Normal:sd(guilt)]^ 2/_b[own]^ 2
```

- -

The `cmxtmixlogit` command invokes Mixed Logit estimation when multiple decisions per subject are available. The call to this function takes as argument the choice variable y, the players' own payoff own, and the variable guilt measuring the expected letdown for each choice alternative. Placing guilt in the random() command option allows ϕ_i to vary randomly following a user-specified parametric distribution (default uses the normal distribution, other parametric distributions are available [StataCorp LLC, 2021]). Output from `cmxtmixlogit` provides the first step reduced-form estimates under the normalization $\lambda = 1$. The `nlcom` commands use these reduced-form estimates to compute structural estimates, following the description presented in Section 4. Standard errors are computed using the Delta method. The online appendix also provides a data file (guiltaversion.dta) containing simulated decisions based on the game in Figure 2, with seven decisions per subject simulated over the set of $z \in \{60, 70, ..., 120\}$. For the simulation, $\phi_i \sim \mathcal{N}(0.7, 0.063)$ and $\lambda = 5$. Player A beliefs that Player B will choose l were drawn from $\mathcal{U}[0, 0.5]$ and independently of z, where $\mathcal{U}[a, b]$ denotes the uniform distribution on the $[a, b]$ interval. These draws were used to construct the variable guilt.

Belief-dependent reciprocity. Dufwenberg and Kirchsteiger (2004) propose a model of belief-dependent reciprocity where the psychological payoff function of player B choosing j is given by the product $PK_i \times K_j$. The first term PK_i captures player B's perception of player A's kindness toward him/her in the game. PK_i is assumed to be negative whenever player B's expected payoff given his/her beliefs about player A's actions and beliefs is below a certain "equitable" payoff, and positive otherwise. Let $\mathbf{E}_i^A \left(\pi_i^B \right)$ denote the material payoff of player B that is expected by player A, conditional on letting player B decide. Moreover, let $\mathbf{E}_i^B \left(\mathbf{E}_i^A \left(\pi_i^B \right) \right)$ denote player B's expectation of $\mathbf{E}_i^A \left(\pi_j^B \right)$. Moreover, define the "equitable" payoff as

$$\pi_i^e = \left(\mathbf{E}_i^B \left(\mathbf{E}_i^A \left(\pi_i^B \right) \right) + \pi_i^B(R) \right) / 2, \tag{39}$$

where $\pi_i^B(R)$ is the outside payoff of player B if player A chooses R in Figure 2. Player B's perceived kindness of player A is given by the following difference

$$PK_i = \mathbf{E}^B \left(\mathbf{E}_i^A \left(\pi_i^B \right) \right) - \pi_i^e. \tag{40}$$

Expected payoffs higher than the equitable payoff are thus perceived as kind. Perceived kindness cannot be negative in the game of Figure 2 given the choice of experimental payoffs for player B. The second term entering the psychological payoff function involves the kindness of player B toward player A for choosing alternative j. Assume that player B's kindness toward player A from choosing alternative j is:

$$K_j = \pi_j^A - \pi_{-j}^A.$$

where $-j$ denotes the other choice alternative. The value function of this model is given by

$$V_{ij} = \pi_{ij} + \phi_i \left[PK_i \times K_j \right] \tag{41}$$
$$= \mathbf{x}_{ij} \boldsymbol{\theta}_i,$$

where

$$\mathbf{x}_{ij} = \left[\pi_{ij}, \left[PK_i \times K_j \right] \right]$$
$$\boldsymbol{\theta}_i = (1, \phi_i)'.$$

Again, akin to the model of simple guilt, psychological payoffs in the model above can be constructed using stated higher-order beliefs, and estimation can proceed following the simple two-step indirect approach outlined above using the constructed psychological payoffs as explanatory variables.

5.3 Measurement of Beliefs and Expectations

The preceding sections outlined the estimation of empirical models of choice under uncertainty using stated belief data. A growing area of research focuses on measurement of expectations and collection of probabilistic data. An early overview of this literature is provided in Manski (2004).

Probabilistic measurement of expectations and beliefs is straightforward when the outcome variable of interest is discrete in nature. In this case, subjects are typically instructed to attribute subjective probabilities to different possible outcomes (see Nyarko and Schotter [2002] for an early example). Measurement of expectations of continuous variables is less straightforward. A simple approach is to ask respondents to report point forecasts of the relevant variables. While this approach is simple, it raises significant issues, some of which relate in particular to the estimation of structural models. First, interpersonal comparisons are complicated by the fact that different points of an underlying subjective distribution (mean, mode, median) may be reported by different respondents. Hence, part of the interpersonal variation of reported point forecasts may simply reflect different interpretations of what the question is trying to elicit. Evidence of this has notably been reported in Engelberg, Manski, and Williams (2009).

Second, point forecasts and estimation of structural models in general do not go hand-in-hand. Point forecasts of a random variable X_{ij} can be used when value functions have the form $V_{ij} = a + bX_{ij}$ where (a, b) are constants, such that $\mathbf{E}(V_{ij}) = a + b\mathbf{E}(X_{ij})$, thus restricting the analysis to models without risk and ambiguity aversion. Inferences would then require replacing $\mathbf{E}(X_{ij})$ by an estimate obtained either by asking respondents to report point forecasts (setting aside problems with such forecasts) or by using other measurement methods described below. Few models in behavioral economics have such a structure. An unattractive alternative would be to assume that subjects face no uncertainty. Then, all subjective distribution would be degenerate and centered around $\mathbf{E}(X_{ij})$ from each subject. This alternative would in effect neutralize many interesting behavioral features including risk and ambiguity.

Probabilistic measurement of expectations in the continuous case proceeds as follows. The range of X_{ij} is first divided in a finite sequence of contiguous intervals. Respondents are asked to state a subjective probability that realizations of X_{ij} will fall within each interval. Intervals can be either common to all respondents, or respondent specific.[37] Stated probabilities can be used to identify a sequence of points on the subjective cumulative distribution function of each respondent. Figure 3 presents an example of a set of points (black circles) for a respondent stating probabilities over 6 intervals spanning $x_{min} = 0$ and $x_{max} = 1$.[38]

Points on the cumulative distribution contain information that can be used to bound measures of central tendency without additional assumptions (see Engelberg, Manski, and Williams, 2009). However, bounds can be large and uninformative prompting different approaches. The parametric approach introduced in Dominitz and Manski (1996) assumes that researchers know the

---

[37] Respondent-specific intervals exploit prior information about the subjective distribution of each respondent in order to concentrate intervals on areas of the domain of X_{ij} that are believed to contain more probability mass. One such source of prior information can be gathered by asking respondents to state subjective min/max values of X_{ij} and define intervals on the basis of this information (see Dominitz, 2001).

[38] In this example, probability mass of $(0.1, 0.1, 0.1, 0.4, 0.2, 0.1)$ was assigned respectively to each of the six intervals.

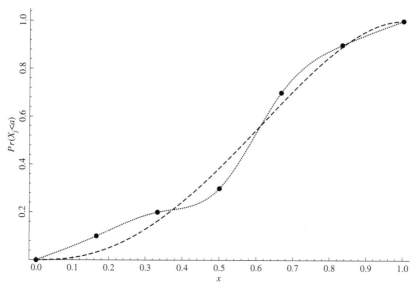

Figure 3 Cumulative distribution functions fitted using the parametric
approach (dashed curve) and cubic spline interpolation (dotted curve). The
parametric approach assumes the subjective distribution of the respondent is a
Beta distribution with unknown parameters (a, b). The distribution fitted using
the parametric approach uses estimated values $(\hat{a} = 2.53, \hat{b} = 1.97)$. Black
circles represent data points.

subjective distribution of each respondent up to a finite vector of parameters.
Beta, triangular, and Gaussian related distributions are typically assumed, with
parameters estimated using nonlinear least squares (see Dominitz and Manski [1996] for an early application to schooling expectations). The dashed
line of Figure 3 presents the fitted curve minimizing the sum of squared
errors assuming a Beta distribution, treating $x_{min} = 0$ and $x_{max} = 1$ as known
parameters. Quantiles and subjective means can be recovered from these
fitted distributions. The parametric approach is simple and intuitive. However, parameter estimates can be unstable and sensitive to starting values,
an indication of the difficulties associated with selecting one or more parametric distributions to fit all respondents in a given sample with a small
number of data points per respondent. Bellemare, Bissonnette, and Kröger
(2012) relax distributional assumptions and fit a cubic spline polynomial to
the data points of each respondent. The dotted line presented in Figure 3
presents the fitted spline. As we can see, the spline interpolation passes through
all data points, exploiting continuity of the assumed distribution over the
range of values. The method delivers a closed-form solution for the fitted
distribution, overcoming numerical problems associated with nonlinear least

squares discussed above.[39] Moreover, Monte Carlo results presented in Belle-mare, Bissonnette, and Kröger (2012) show that cubic spline interpolation is substantially less affected by rounding of probabilistic responses than the parametric approach. Rounding is a prominent form of non-standard measurement error which leads to probabilistic responses bunched at specific focal values (multiples of 5 and 10 in particular).[40] For these reasons, the spline interpolation offers a flexible and robust approach to model subjective probability distributions in the case of continuous outcome variables.

Probabilistic measurement of expectations for continuous outcomes is now frequently applied in many areas of economics.[41] However, few applications of this approach have appeared in experimental economics. Bellemare, Bissonnette, and Kröger (2010) are perhaps the first to apply this approach using experimental data, focusing on data from a binary trust game. They model sender behavior as a function of the monetary benefits of trusting or not the other player (the amount senders expect to receive if they trust or not) and the utility value of creating a surplus by investing (efficiency concerns). Expectations were collected by breaking down the ranges of possible amounts returned when trusting and not trusting in six intervals each.[42] and subjects in the role of senders were asked to state probabilities for each of these intervals. Another recent application is Breunig et al. (2021), who measure expectations of equity returns using probabilistic belief data in combination with spline interpolation. The fitted splines are used to analyze the portfolio choice problem using data from a large-scale experiment in Germany.

The fitted distributions using any of the approaches discussed above can be used to estimate $\mathbf{E}(V_{ij})$. Perhaps the simplest way to proceed is to use simulation-based methods (see Train, 2009) and approximate $\mathbf{E}(V_{ij})$ by averaging V_{ij} using a sequence of *i.i.d.* draws from the fitted distribution of each respondent. Structural parameters of the model would then be estimated conditional on these draws.[43] The estimation of structural models using fitted subjective distributions of continuous random variables is still in its infancy. Recent papers in other areas of economics have relied on point forecasts (e.g.

---

[39] The file **beliefs.do** in the online appendix illustrates how to use the Stata `splineBBK` function to fit subjective distributions using data from proposers in the binary trust game of Bellemare, Bissonnette, and Kröger (2010).

[40] See Manski and Molinari (2010).

[41] The *Journal of Econometrics* recently published a special issue covering a broad range of applications (see Delavande, van der Klaauw, Winter, and Zafar, 2022).

[42] The design allowed players to return an amount from their initial endowment even if senders chose not to trust.

[43] The online appendix provides the Stata .ado file `splineBBK` implementing spline interpolation. The file can also be used to generate random draws from the fitted subjective distributions.

see Delavande and Zafar, 2019), neglecting the uncertainty facing decision-makers. Exploiting the entire information available about the uncertainty of respondents about a continuous random variable in the context of structural estimation is an interesting yet largely unexplored area of research.

Finally, the elicitation procedure requires that subjects state probabilities for well-defined probability distributions. As discussed in Section 5.2, models of ambiguity question the capacity of individuals to form and act on well-defined subjective probability distributions over the different possible states of the world. Yet, subjects facing ambiguity may nevertheless provide well-defined distributions when asked to do so using the elicitation procedures above. Providing proper subjective distribution does not guarantee that subjects make decisions on the basis of these distributions. Early research on the impact of ambiguity on elicited probability distributions suggests that prominence of stated responses of "50%" for binary outcomes may be an expression of ambiguity (Bruine de et al., 2000). Bellemare, Kröger, and Sossou (2018) find that experimental subjects contemplating a fixed set of possible distributions will tend to report well-defined probability distributions when asked, and will generally do so by weighing possible distributions according to their perceived subjective likelihoods.

Measuring ambiguity is an emerging research area. One approach has been to allow respondents to state a range of probabilities rather than a precise probability for a given event (see Giustinelli, Manski, and Molinari, 2020), consistent with the idea that subjects hold beliefs about sets of subjective distributions rather than about a single subjective distribution. Estimation of structural models integrating such information is an interesting avenue of future research.

5.4 Endogeneity of Stated Beliefs

In most models of choice under risk and uncertainty, individuals are endowed with preferences and beliefs which are combined with possibly other factors (for example decision-making errors) to determine choices. While preferences and beliefs are often treated as two distinct objects, it appears plausible that both can be correlated at the individual level. Endogeneity of stated higher-order beliefs in models with belief-dependent preferences (e.g. see (38) and (41)) is frequently debated. In these models, nonselfish players may guess that other players believe nonselfish behavior is a norm and thus state higher-order beliefs correlated with their own preferences. Alternatively, they may form expectations placing an important weight on their own behavior and preferences. Even if preferences and true underling beliefs are independent, empirical analysis relies on stated, rather than true, beliefs. Recent work suggests that the way beliefs are elicited may introduce various patterns of endogeneity (see Bauer and Wol, 2018).

Taking into account endogeneity of stated beliefs is essential to obtain consistent estimates of the model parameters. Experimental methods offer interesting means to tackle endogeneity of stated beliefs. Several papers have recently implemented designs intended to exogenously shift or "set" beliefs of players. Costa-Gomes, Huck, and Weizsäcker (2014) randomly shift the return shares of responders in a continuous trust game. They exploit instrumental variable techniques and find that beliefs in the game have a causal impact of choices of proposers. Khalmetski (2016) induces similar exogenous shifts in second-order beliefs to test for guilt aversion. Ellingsen et al. (2010) argue that endogeneity of stated higher-order beliefs may bias upward estimates of guilt aversion. To test this assumption they propose a new experimental design where relevant players are provided the first-order beliefs of the players they are matched with in the game. In such a design, the second-order beliefs of the relevant players are exogenously "set" to those of their matched players. They find that estimated guilt aversion is significantly weakened when beliefs are set exogenously. These results are interpreted as evidence that stated higher-order beliefs are endogenous. With that said, exogenously setting beliefs by passing along stated beliefs of other players raises some issues and concerns as this may trigger alternative behavioral responses beyond guilt aversion.[44]

The papers above tackle the issue of endogeneity using experimental methods combined with reduced-form regression techniques. Structural models estimated using experimental data and controlling for potential endogeneity of stated beliefs are scarce. Bellemare, Kröger, and Van Soest (2008a) jointly model stated beliefs and choices of senders in the ultimatum game, controlling for possible correlation between Fehr and Schmidt (1999) preferences and stated beliefs. They find that inequity aversion to having less is positively and significantly correlated with optimism – the likelihood of stating a higher probability that a given offer is accepted. Bellemare, Sebald, and Strobel (2008) exploit data from a binary trust game with two treatments to recover estimates of guilt aversion in a large sample of the Dutch population. The first experimental treatment requires that subjects state higher-order beliefs, where stated

---

[44] Battigalli and Dufwenberg (2020) point out that Ellingsen et al. (2010) do not reveal to players that their beliefs will be passed on to others, and this information is shared with the receiving players. The latter may then question whether some design features were also hidden from them, affecting their behavior. Bellemare, Sebald, and Suetens (2017) find that the design of Ellingsen et al. (2010) induces a strong unconditional increase in kindness that is not related to belief-dependent preferences.

beliefs are possibly endogenous. The second treatment implements the design of Ellingsen et al. (2010) discussed above, passing along first-order beliefs of relevant players in order to exogenously set or fix expectations. They jointly model choices and stated beliefs in both experimental treatments and estimate their model using Maximum Likelihood. They find that the estimated level of guilt aversion is significantly higher when using stated higher-order beliefs relative to exogenously setting beliefs as in Ellingsen et al. (2010). More importantly, they find that the gap between these estimates is fully explained by an estimated positive correlation between stated beliefs and unobserved preferences. Recently, Bellemare and Sebald (2022) show how to bound the importance of guilt aversion and belief-dependent preferences in a RUM setting when data on beliefs are not available. Their approach exploits data from a subset of games where these preferences are ruled-out by construction. Data from these games are used to estimate non-parametrically the distribution of errors in a RUM. Conditional on this distribution, bounds can be recovered in games where guilt aversion and belief-dependent reciprocity may play a role, exploiting the fact that psychological payoffs for each preference functional (see (38) and (41)) are interval-measured and independent of beliefs.

Jointly modeling choices and beliefs will in general require programming. A simpler two-step "control function" approach is possible which can be implemented using basic estimation commands. The following draws on Train (2009), who provides an excellent overview of approaches to deal with endogeneity in structural discrete choice models. Consider the following simple random utility model:

$$\begin{aligned}
\tilde{V}_{ij} &= V_{ij} + \lambda \varepsilon_{ij} \\
&= b_{ij}\theta_i + \lambda \varepsilon_{ij},
\end{aligned} \tag{42}$$

where b_{ij} is an explanatory variable which is a function of the stated beliefs of subject i for choice j. Here, b_{ij} could be one of the psychological payoff functions discussed previously (see (38) and (41)), or a subjective expected valuation for alternative j.[45] The approach requires specification of a secondary equation

$$b_{ij} = f(z_{ij}, \gamma) + v_{ij}, \tag{43}$$

where z_{ij} is an instrumental variable independent of ε_{ij} and v_{ij}. Endogeneity arises in this model because the latter two random terms are correlated,

---

[45] The control function approach does not require V_{ij} to be a linear function of the endogenous explanatory variable, see Train (2009). However, most of the models in this paper have such a structure.

which implies that b_{ij} is correlated with ε_{ij} in the primary equation (42). This correlation can be captured by decomposing ε_{ij} as the sum of a control function $C(v_{ij}, \phi)$ and a mean-zero residual $\tilde{\varepsilon}_{ij}$. If the control function was known, then it could simply be added to equation (42) as an additional explanatory variable, in effect purging ε_{ij} of its correlation with b_{ij}. There is some degree of flexibility when choosing the control function. Perhaps the simplest functional form is given by $C(v_{ij}, \phi) = \phi v_{ij}$ (for other functional forms, see Train [2009]). This leads to the following augmented value function model:

$$\tilde{V}_{ij} = V_{ij} + \lambda \varepsilon_{ij}$$
$$= b_{ij}\theta_i + \lambda \phi v_{ij} + \lambda \tilde{\varepsilon}_{ij}.$$

In practice, $C(v_{ij}, \phi)$ is not known but can be consistently estimated in a first step. In particular, estimates $\hat{v}_{ij}$ can be recovered from estimation of the secondary equation (43). The control function $C(\hat{v}_{ij}, \phi)$ can be constructed using $\hat{v}_{ij}$ and all remaining parameters in (42) can be estimated in a second step. Standard errors of the second step estimates can be computed using bootstrap procedures.[46]

A treatment dummy variable capturing exogenous shifts in beliefs as implemented in the design of Costa-Gomes, Huck, and Weizsäcker (2014) could serve as the instrumental variable z_{ij}. Note that setting beliefs as in Ellingsen et al. (2010) does not require using the two-step indirect approach described above. This follows because setting beliefs exogenously guarantees that b_{ij} is independent of ε_{ij}. Estimation of the model using data from this design can be accomplished in a single step given b_{ij} can be treated like any other exogenous explanatory variable. As mentioned previously, setting beliefs in such a way raises other concerns (see footnote 44).

6 Model Validation

Model validation is an important step to convince both researchers and readers that a given structural model can explain observed behavior well. Model validation can be conducted both within-sample and out-of-sample. Within-sample validation amounts to computing goodness-of fit measures based on all observations that were used in the estimation of the model parameters. Validation usually begins by comparing candidate models on the basis of general within-sample goodness-of-fit measures including the log-likelihood function value, (pseudo) r-squares, etc. There are some shortcomings when comparing models on the basis of general goodness-of-fit measures. First, general within-sample

---

[46] All steps can be carried out using built-in commands in Stata.

goodness-of-fit measures may be useful to identify a better fitting model, but they do not reveal which subset of the data is well fitted, and which is not. Comparing the actual choice distribution with the corresponding distribution predicted using a given model provides more information about possible model misspecifications. Such comparisons can also be conducted for various subsets of subjects to assess model fit along specific dimensions (e.g. age, gender, treatment).

Mixed Logit with Fehr and Schmidt (1999) preferences - Stata example cntd (`discrete.do`)

```
margins if decision == 1
```

Section 4.2 presented code for Mixed Logit estimation of the distribution of Fehr and Schmidt (1999) preferences using the `cmxtmixlogit` command applied to simulated data on responder behavior in the ultimatum game. Assessing model fit post-estimation can be accomplished using the `margins` command above which allows to predict choice probabilities which can be compared to actual choice probabilities in order to assess within-sample model fit. In the example command line above, the predicted distribution of acceptance rates for responders is generated for the first decision (offer) received using the `if` option. Predicted distributions can also be generated for various subsets of subjects along observable dimensions (e.g. gender) using the `if` option.

Second, maximization of general within-sample goodness-of-fit measures is not always desirable. For example, the number of classes in a population is an important quantity to estimate in finite mixture models (see Section 4.2). Maximization of goodness-of-fit would lead researchers to add as many classes as numerically possible. However, inferences on the number of classes based on comparisons of the log-likelihood function value is not straightforward. In particular, the distribution of the log-likelihood ratio test under the null hypothesis about a given number of classes is not a standard chi-square distribution (see McLachlan, Lee, and Rathnayake, 2019, sec. 6.4). This explains why researchers tend to determine class size using other approaches. The most popular approach in behavioral economic applications has been to use information criteria. These criteria have the form $-2LL + \psi K$, where LL denotes the log-likelihood function value of a model with a given number of classes and corresponding number of model parameters K, and ψ controls the size of the penalty associated with the number of parameters estimated for a given class size. AIC ($\psi = 2$) and BIC ($\psi = \ln(N)$, with N the sample size). Here, the selection of classes thus balances within-sample goodness of fit (captured by LL) with a penalty for the number of model parameters. Research using Monte Carlo simulations to evaluate the performance of information criteria to correctly identify class sizes in finite mixture models is inconclusive. AIC may be preferred over BIC (or vice versa) depending on the sample size, number of classes in the population, and number of variables entering the model (see Grimm, Houpt, and Rodgers [2021] for a recent review). Using information criteria may also help limit the specification and estimation of overfitted models. Overfitting occurs when increasing the number of model parameters of an economic model leads to noise in decision-making being incorrectly attributed to the (overly complex) economic model that is fitted. Given noise may vary across treatments or subjects, overfitted models that have a very good within-sample fit may perform poorly in an out-of-sample validation exercise. It follows that conducting an out-of-sample validation exercise using a holdout sample may be useful to identify potential problems due to overfitting.[47]

An interesting application of within-sample goodness-of-fit is Bajari and Hortacsu (2005). They focus on evaluating the credibility of structural models of bidding behavior using experimental data from laboratory auctions. A salient feature of these models is that they maintain strong rationality assumptions about bidding behavior in order to recover estimates of private valuations for the goods auctioned. The plausibility of these estimates thus relies on the credibility of the underlying assumptions of these models. In contrast to field data, experimental data from laboratory auctions contain the private valuations that were randomly assigned to bidders. Bajari and Hortacsu (2005) compare the distribution of private valuations in experiments to those estimated using a class of structural models. Their analysis exploits experimental auction data published by Dyer, Kagel, and Levin (1989). By and large they find that the distribution of private valuations recovered from structural auction models is consistent with those randomly assigned to bidders in the experiments. They further analyze behavioral models of bidding behavior relaxing some rationality assumptions and find that such models fit better the randomly assigned valuations. This example illustrates the value of experiments for model validation. Here, private valuations are not observable in nonexperimental auction data. As such, the same model validation exercise conducted in Bajari and Hortacsu (2005) could not be undertaken without experimental data.

---

[47] See Lever, Krzywinski, and Altman (2016), who present a particularly clear and insightful discussion of the value of using holdout-samples to detect overfitting.

The preceding example highlighted within-sample goodness-of-fit. However, because many model estimates are obtained by maximizing an objective function which already seeks to bridge the gap between predicted and observed behavior within-sample (through Maximum Likelihood estimation, Method-of-moments estimation, etc.), within-sample goodness-of-fit is not the most stringent validation exercise. Out-of-sample validation, on the other hand, is a more demanding and revealing exercise. There, a holdout sample is constructed by removing a portion of the sample during estimation. Model estimates obtained using the remaining data are subsequently used to predict behavior in the hold-out sample.

It is particularly insightful to construct an experimental hold-out sample that differs from the estimation sample with respect to some of the key elements of the choice environment that are analyzed. Duflo, Hanna, and Ryan (2012) analyzed data from a controlled field experiment in India aimed at reducing teacher absenteeism through the use of financial incentives. In the experiment, schools were randomly assigned to baseline and treatment conditions. Treatments conditions provided financial incentives for teachers to increase attendance. The incentives were provided by offering (1) a bonus for each additional day of attendance in a given month in excess of 20 days (the cutoff monthly attendance), and (2) a fine for each day of absence when the total number of days of presence is below 20 days per month. They estimated several specifications of their structural model using (a) full information Maximum Likelihood, and (b) Simulated Method of Moments. In all cases, estimation was conducted using treatment school data only, exploiting within month variations of the marginal benefits and costs of additional days of attendance. This allowed researchers to perform out-of-sample predictions of the attendance rates in schools assigned to control conditions. Moreover, Simulated Method of Moments estimation exploited only the first few days of each calendar month, providing an additional out-of-sample prediction exercise for the remaining days of each month. Duflo, Hanna, and Ryan (2012) were able to identify specifications that perform well in these out-of-sample exercises. They subsequently performed several counterfactual policy simulations to identify optimal incentives schedules not used in the field experiment, but which would further increase attendance without raising costs. These optimal schedules differed from the experimental schedule with respect to monthly attendance cutoffs and bonus sizes.

It is also important to emphasize there are settings where a good within-sample fit is necessary but not sufficient to validate a behavioral model. Conducting an additional out-of-sample validation exercise may then be particularly useful. This is especially true when experimental choice data are not rich enough to identify all model components. As discussed in Section 5.2, Manski (2002) makes the case that many combinations of preferences and beliefs can be consistent with the same choice data in economic experiments of proposal and response. This identification problem has additional implications for the value of within-sample model validation. In particular, if two (or more) models can explain equally well the same data, then within-sample goodness of fit is likely to be similar across the different models fitted to the data. Put differently, good within-sample fit is *not* sufficient to validate a model. This issue is illustrated in Bellemare, Kröger, and Van Soest (2008a) (see discussion in Section 5.2). They compare the within-sample and out-of-sample predictive power of a model of choice under uncertainty (proposers in the ultimatum game) estimated using elicited subjective probabilities with a model estimated assuming subjects have rational expectations. Within-sample goodness-of-fit was found to be good and very similar for both models - a reflection of the identification problem outlined above. An out-of-sample goodness-of-fit exercise was additionally conducted using holdout sample data from a dictator game ran with different subjects in conjunction to the ultimatum game experiment. This dictator game experiment was isomorphic to their implementation of the ultimatum game (same choice set, incentives, subject pool), but removed uncertainty about the behavior of responders (setting $Q_{ij} = 1$ in equation 37). Estimates of each model were used to predict the offer distribution in the dictator game, the out-of-sample predictions. There, the model using subjective probabilistic data provided a significantly better fit than the model imposing rational expectations. It followed that an out-of-sample goodness-of-fit analysis was necessary to validate and invalidate the different models that were estimated in that paper.

To summarize, within-sample goodness-of-fit model validation is a necessary but in general insufficient to validate a model, as high within-sample fit may reflect overfitting or inappropriate handling of decision-making errors. The examples discussed above demonstrate that the value of an out-of-sample validation exercise go beyond avoiding problems of overfitting. More importantly, experimental methods can be used to implement changes in the choice environment whose effects can be predicted by a well-specified structural model. Changes in the choice environment of interest on the other hand are not always present in nonexperimental data. For example, a structural model may be specified and estimated to predict the effect of a counterfactual policy or intervention not yet implemented. Experiments allow researchers to collect data under various treatment interventions and thus offer the opportunity to perform a relevant out-of-sample validation exercise.

7 Conclusion

Laboratory or field experiments allow researchers to exogenously vary the choice environment of subjects through the implementation of experimental treatments. Accordingly, the econometric analysis of experimental data has up to now predominantly relied on reduced-form approaches focused on measuring and detecting treatment effects. However, behavioral theoretical models are increasingly available to explain choice data in experiments. Bringing thee models to data is essential to understand their strengths and limitations. Documenting the latter is essential to build a new generation of models which better predict behavior.

It has been argued that the choice of empirical approach to data analysis, whether reduced-form or structural should be dictated by the research question that is addressed. Research questions focused on identification of specific decision rules (preferences and beliefs) and their possible heterogeneity in the population would benefit from structural approaches. It is important to emphasize the need to determine which empirical approach to pursue before designing and running experiments. A design that is well powered to detect treatments effects may not be adequate to detect a plurality of decision rules in a population with sufficiently high sampling probability. Moreover, separate identification of all features of a structural model may require a specific experimental design (such as gathering multiple decisions per subjects). The experimental design in Bellemare, Kröger, and Sossou (2020), for example, was the result of a large number of Monte Carlo simulations conducted over several months to guarantee (ex ante) that the experimental design could be used to separately identify all components of the structural model (loss, risk, and ambiguity aversion). Such examples demonstrate the importance of approaching the design of economic experiments with a different mind set if structural estimation is to be undertaken.

The paper provided examples (e.g. Shearer, 2004) where experimental methods enrich structural modeling by reducing the level of assumptions that would otherwise be imposed to make model estimation feasible. Experimental methods also provide means to validate models by contrasting predicted behavior with experimental data or design parameters (e.g. Bajari and Hortacsu, 2005; Duflo, Hanna, and Ryan, 2012). For these reasons, the synergies between experiments and structural modeling offer interesting research opportunities. As was discussed in the paper, there is some work estimating structural models of decision-making under ambiguity, but much more needs to be done. The challenge here is gathering information about the ambiguity facing decisions makers and using this subjective information to estimate and compare models.

Here, the benefits of being able to design an experiment for that particular purpose are clear.

The Element has also shown that many well-established models in behavioral economics can be estimated using standard statistical software with little or no programming efforts. The online appendix offers Stata code for many of the models discussed to facilitate adoption. However, estimation of more complex models (e.g. those with multiple nonnested preferences in the population) will require independent programming skills. This in turn will require expanding the programming base of experimental economists. Fortunately, past publication outcomes of papers surveyed here suggest the returns to building up such skills may be high.

8 Content of Online Appendix

The online appendix provides Stata code which can be used to implement structural estimation of some well-known models in behavioral economics covered in the paper. The codes and examples provided do not require any programming skills. Instead, basic understanding of built-in Stata commands is required. Estimation of more complex models will in general require programming; the latter can be done in many different programming languages which provide users with optimisation routines.

The codes and data files provided include:

pamodel.do: implements estimation of a principal agent model with and without reciprocal preferences. Subsets of this code are presented and discussed in Section 2 of the paper. File `pamodel.dta` contains simulated data of worker behavior as a function of randomly assigned piece-rates and gifts from the firm. The data-generating process used to simulate worker output y_{ij} over 30 periods is the following:

$$\log\left(y_{ij}\right) = \alpha_0 + \gamma \log\left(r_j + \beta_i G_{ij}\right) + \alpha_i + \varepsilon_{ij}$$

where $G_{ij} = 1$ for 15 periods, $r_j \in \{0.16, 0.18, 0.2\}$ for 10 periods each, and

$$\alpha_0 = 6$$

$$\gamma = 0.5$$

$$\beta_i = 1 + 0.5x_i$$

$$x_i \quad \sim \mathcal{U}[0,2]$$

$$\alpha_i \quad \sim \mathcal{N}(1,0.25)$$

$$\varepsilon_{ij} \quad \sim \mathcal{N}(0,0.25),$$

where $\mathcal{U}[a,b]$ represents the uniform distribution on the interval $[a,b]$ and $\mathcal{N}(c,d)$ represents the normal distribution with mean c and variance d.

altruism.do: Implements nonlinear least squares and Maximum Likelihood two-limit Tobit model based on first-order conditions derived from the CES utility function of Andreoni and Miller (2002) discussed in Section 3. Standard errors are computed using the delta method.

discrete.do: Implements Conditional Logit and Mixed Logit estimation of the Fehr and Schmidt (1999) model using simulated data from responders in the ultimatum game with Fehr and Schmidt (1999) preferences $((\alpha_i, \beta_i)$ values, see Section 4.3). Estimation is conducted on the two-step indirect approach outlined in Section 4. The code allows users to compare estimates obtained using one or more decisions per subjects. The data file `responders.dta` contains data from the simulation. The data-generating process used to simulate decisions is the following :

$$\alpha_i = 0.5 + u_i^\alpha \text{ where } u_i^\alpha \sim \mathcal{N}(0, 0.5)$$
$$\beta_i = 0.3 + u_i^\beta \text{ where } u_i^\alpha \sim \mathcal{N}(0, 0.5)$$
$$\lambda = 0.5$$
$$Corr(u_i^\alpha, u_i^\beta) = 0.5,$$

where $\mathcal{N}(c,d)$ represents the normal distribution with mean c and variance d. The sample contains 10 decisions for each responder, one for each of the 10 possible offers, akin to a design using the strategy method.

guiltaversion.do: Implements Mixed Logit estimation of the model of simple guilt of Battigalli and Dufwenberg (2007) using simulated data from a binary trust game and based on the two-step indirect approach outlined in Section 4. The data file `guiltaversion.dta` contains data from simulated decisions of subjects with guilt averse preferences defined by a sensitivity parameter (ϕ_i). These decisions were simulated over the set of $z \in \{60, 70, ..., 120\}$ of pay-offs presented in Figure 2 of the paper. The data-generating process used for the simulation is $\phi_i \sim \mathcal{N}(0.7, 0.063)$ and $\lambda = 5$, where $\mathcal{N}(c,d)$ represents the normal distribution with mean c and variance d. Player A beliefs that Player B will choose l were drawn from $\mathcal{U}[0, 0.5]$ and independently of z, where $\mathcal{U}[a,b]$ represents the uniform distribution on the interval $[a,b]$. The sample contains 7 decisions per subject, one for each value z.

beliefs.do: Implements cubic spline interpolation using the Stata `splineBBK` command discussed in Section 5. Code is applied to the data file (`beliefs .dta`) containing proposer decisions in the binary trust game of Bellemare,

Bissonnette, and Kröger (2012). Data on probabilistic beliefs of proposers are included. These data cover a sequence of contiguous intervals regarding the amount of money they expected responders to return under two scenarios (investing or not their endowment).

References

Abdellaoui, M. (2000). "Parameter-free elicitation of utility and probability weighting functions," *Management Science*, 46(11), 1497–1512.

Adeline Delavande and Wilbert van der Klaauw and Joachim Winter and Basit Zafar (2022). Introduction to the Journal of Econometrics Annals Issue on "Subjective Expectations and Probabilities in Economics," *Journal of Econometrics*, 231(1), 1–2.

Ahn, D., S. Choi, D. Gale, and S. Kariv (2014). "Estimating ambiguity aversion in a portfolio choice experiment," *Quantitative Economics*, 5(2), 195–223.

Akerlof, G. A. (1982). "Labor contracts as partial gift exchange," *The Quarterly Journal of Economics*, 97(4), 543–569.

Andersen, S., G. W. Harrison, M. I. Lau, and E. E. Rutström (2008). "Eliciting risk and time preferences," *Econometrica*, 76(3), 583–618.

Andreoni, J., and J. Miller (2002). "Giving according to GARP, an experimental test of the consistency of preferences for altruism," *Econometrica*, 70, 737–753.

Apesteguia, J., and M. A. Ballester (2018). "Monotone stochastic choice models: The case of risk and time preferences," *Journal of Political Economy*, 126(1), 74–106.

Baillon, A., and H. Bleichrodt (2015). "Testing ambiguity models through the measurement of probabilities for gains and losses," *American Economic Journal: Microeconomics*, 7(2), 77–100.

Bajari, P., and A. Hortacsu (2005). "Are structural estimates of auction models reasonable? Evidence from experimental data," *Journal of Political Economy*, 113(4), 703–741.

Bardsley, N., and P. G. Moffatt (2007). "The experimetrics of public goods: Inferring motivations from contributions," *Theory and Decision*, 62(2), 161–193.

Barsky, R. B., F. T. Juster, M. S. Kimball, and M. D. Shapiro (1997). "Preference parameters and behavioral heterogeneity: An experimental approach in the health and retirement study," *The Quarterly Journal of Economics*, 112(2), 537–579.

Batley, R. (2008). "On ordinal utility, cardinal utility and random utility," *Theory and Decision*, 64(1), 37–63.

Battigalli, P., and M. Dufwenberg (2007). "Guilt in games," *American Economic Review*, 97(2), 170–176.

(2022). "Belief-dependent motivations and psychological game theory," *Journal of Economic Literature*, 60(3), 833–882.

Bauer, D., and I. Wol (2018). "Biases in beliefs: Experimental evidence," *TWI Research Paper Series*, No. 109.

Bellemare, C., L. Bissonnette, and S. Kröger (2010). "Bounding preference parameters under different assumptions about beliefs: A partial identification approach," *Experimental Economics*, 13(3), 334–345.

(2012). "Flexible approximation of subjective expectations using probability questions," *Journal of Business and Economic Statistics*, 30, 125–131.

Bellemare, C., S. Kröger, and K. M. Sossou (2018). "Reporting probabilistic expectations with dynamic uncertainty about possible distributions," *Journal of Risk and Uncertainty*, 57(2), 153–176.

(2020). "Optimal frequency of portfolio evaluation in a choice experiment with ambiguity and loss aversion," *Journal of Econometrics* Vol. 231, Issue 1, November 2022, 248–264.

Bellemare, C., S. Kröger, and A. van Soest (2008a). "Measuring inequity aversion in a heterogeneous population using experimental decisions and subjective probabilities," *Econometrica*, 76, 815–839.

(2008b). "Preferences, intentions, and expectations violations: A large-scale experiment with a representative subject pool," *Journal of Economic Behavior and Organization*, 78, 349–365.

Bellemare, C., and A. Sebald (2022). "Measuring belief-dependent preferences without data on beliefs," *Review of Economic Studies, forthcoming* 0034–6527, https://doi.org/10.1093/restud/rdac023.

Bellemare, C., A. Sebald, and M. Strobel (2008). "Measuring the willingness to pay to avoid guilt: Estimation using equilibrium and stated belief models," *Journal of Applied Econometrics*, 26, 437–453.

Bellemare, C., A. Sebald, and S. Suetens (2017). "A note on testing guilt aversion," *Games and Economic Behavior*, 102, 233–239.

(2018). "Heterogeneous guilt sensitivities and incentive effects," *Experimental Economics*, 21(2), 316–336.

Bellemare, C., and B. Shearer (2009). "Gift giving and worker productivity: Evidence from a firm level experiment," *Games and Economic Behavior*, 67, 233–244.

(2011). "On the relevance and composition of gifts within the firm: Evidence from field experiments," *International Economic Review*, 52, 855–882.

Berg, J., J. Dickhaut, and K. McCabe (1995). "Trust, reciprocity, and social history," *Games and Economic Behavior*, 10(1), 122–142.

Bolton, G. E., and A. Ockenfels (2000). "ERC: A theory of equity, reciprocity, and competition," *American Economic Review*, 90(1), 166–193.

Brandts, J., and G. Charness (2011). "The strategy versus the direct-response method: A first survey of experimental comparisons," *Experimental Economics*, 14(3), 375–398.

Breunig, C., S. Huck, T. Schmidt, and G. Weizsäcker (2021). "The standard portfolio choice problem in Germany," *The Economic Journal,* Vol. 131, Issue 638, August 2021, 2413–2446.

Bruhin, A., E. Fehr, and D. Schunk (2019). "The many faces of human sociality: Uncovering the distribution and stability of social preferences," *Journal of the European Economic Association*, 17(4), 1025–1069.

Bruhin, A., H. Fehr-Duda, and T. Epper (2010). "Risk and rationality: Uncovering heterogeneity in probability distortion," *Econometrica*, 78(4), 1375–1412.

Bruine de Bruin, W., B. Fischhoff, B. Halpern-Felsher, and S. Millstein (2000). "Expressing epistemic uncertainty: It's a fifty-fifty chance," *Organizational Behavior and Human Decision Processes*, 81(1), 115–131.

Bruyn, A. D., and G. E. Bolton (2008). "Estimating the influence of fairness on bargaining behavior," *Management Science*, 54, 1774–1791.

Camerer, C. F., and T.-H. Ho (1994). "Violations of the betweenness axiom and nonlinearity in probability," *Journal of Risk and Uncertainty*, 8(2), 167–196.

Cappelen, A., A. D. Hole, E. Sørensen, and B. Tundoggen (2007). "The pluralism of fairness ideals: An experimental approach," *American Economic Review*, 97, 818–827.

Charness, G., and M. Rabin (2002). "Understanding social preferences with simple tests," *The Quarterly Journal of Economics*, 117(3), 817–869.

Conte, A., and J. D. Hey (2013). "Assessing multiple prior models of behaviour under ambiguity," *Journal of Risk and Uncertainty*, 46(2), 113–132.

Conte, A., J. D. Hey, and P. G. Moffatt (2011). "Mixture models of choice under risk," *Journal of Econometrics*, 162, 79–88.

Conte, A., and P. Moffatt (2014). "The econometric modelling of social preferences," *Theory and Decision*, 76, 119–145.

Conte, A., P. G. Moffatt, F. Botti, D. T. Di Cagno, and C. d'Ippoliti (2012). "A test of the rational expectations hypothesis using data from a natural experiment," *Applied Economics*, 44(35), 4661–4678.

Costa-Gomes, M. A., S. Huck, and G. Weizsäcker (2014). "Beliefs and actions in the trust game: Creating instrumental variables to estimate the causal effect," *Games and Economic Behavior*, 88, 298–309.

Cox, J. C. (2004). "How to identify trust and reciprocity," *Games and Economic Behavior*, 46(2), 260–281.

Cox, J. C., D. Friedman, and S. Gjerstad (2007). "A tractable model of reciprocity and fairness," *Games and Economic Behavior*, 59(1), 17–45.

Cubitt, R., G. Van De Kuilen, and S. Mukerji (2020). "Discriminating between models of ambiguity attitude: A qualitative test," *Journal of the European Economic Association*, 18(2), 708–749.

Delavande, A., and B. Zafar (2019). "University choice: The role of expected earnings, nonpecuniary outcomes, and financial constraints," *Journal of Political Economy*, 127(5), 2343–2393.

DellaVigna, S. (2018). "Structural behavioral economics," in B. D. Bernheim, S. DellaVigna, and D. Laibson (eds.), *Handbook of behavioral economics: Applications and foundations 1*, vol. 1, pp. 613–723. Elsevier.

Dominitz, J. (2001). "Estimation of income expectations models using expectations and realization data," *Journal of Econometrics*, 102(2), 165–195.

Dominitz, J., and C. F. Manski (1996). "Eliciting student expectations of the returns to schooling," *Journal of Human Resources*, vol. 31 1–26.

Duflo, E., R. Hanna, and S. P. Ryan (2012). "Incentives work: Getting teachers to come to school," *American Economic Review*, 102(4), 1241–1278.

Dufwenberg, M., and G. Kirchsteiger (2004). "A theory of sequential reciprocity," *Games and Economic Behavior*, 47(2), 268–298.

Dyer, D., J. H. Kagel, and D. Levin (1989). "Resolving uncertainty about the number of bidders in independent private-value auctions: An experimental analysis," *The RAND Journal of Economics*, vol. 20 268–279.

Ellingsen, T., M. Johannesson, S. Tjøtta, and G. Torsvik (2010). "Testing guilt aversion," *Games and Economic Behavior*, 68(1), 95–107.

Ellsberg, D. (1961). "Risk, ambiguity, and the savage axioms," *The Quarterly Journal of Economics*, vol. 75 643–669.

Engelberg, J., C. F. Manski, and J. Williams (2009). "Comparing the point predictions and subjective probability distributions of professional forecasters," *Journal of Business & Economic Statistics*, 27(1), 30–41.

Engelmann, D., and M. Strobel (2004). "Inequality aversion, efficiency, and maximin preferences in simple distribution experiments," *American Economic Review*, 94(4), 857–869.

Fechner, G. T. (1860). *Elemente der psychophysik*, vol. 2. Breitkopf & Härtel.

Fehr, E., G. Kirchsteiger, and A. Riedl (1993). "Does fairness prevent market clearing? An experimental investigation," *The Quarterly Journal of Economics*, 108(2), 437–459.

Fehr, E., and K. M. Schmidt (1999). "A theory of fairness, competition, and cooperation," *The Quarterly Journal of Economics*, 114(3), 817–868.

Gilboa, I., and D. Schmeidler (1989). "Maxmin expected utility with non-unique prior," *Journal of Mathematical Economics*, 18(2), 141–153.

Giustinelli, P., C. F. Manski, and F. Molinari (2022). "Precise or imprecise probabilities? Evidence from survey response related to late-onset dementia," *Journal of the European Economic Association* vol. 20, pp. 187–221.

Gneezy, U., and J. A. List (2006). "Putting behavioral economics to work: Testing for gift exchange in labor markets using field experiments," *Econometrica*, 74(5), 1365–1384.

Goldstein, W. M., and H. J. Einhorn (1987). "Expression theory and the preference reversal phenomena," *Psychological Review*, 94(2), pp. 236–254.

Greene, W. H. (2003). *Econometric analysis*, 8th ed. Pearson Education India. (2017). *Econometric analysis*, 8th ed. Pearson Education India.

Grimm KJ, Houpt R and Rodgers D (2021) Model Fit and Comparison in Finite Mixture Models: A Review and a Novel Approach. Front. Educ. 6:613645. doi: 10.3389/feduc.2021.613645

Hey, J. D., G. Lotito, and A. Maffioletti (2010). "The descriptive and predictive adequacy of theories of decision making under uncertainty/ambiguity," *Journal of Risk and Uncertainty*, 41(2), 81–111.

Hey, J. D., and C. Orme (1994). "Investigating generalizations of expected utility theory using experimental data," *Econometrica: Journal of the Econometric Society*, vol. 62 1291–1326.

Holt, C. A., and S. K. Laury (2002). "Risk aversion and incentive effects," *American Economic Review*, 92(5), 1644–1655. (2014). "Assessment and estimation of risk preferences," in M. J. Machina and W. K. Viscusi (eds.), *Handbook of the economics of risk and uncertainty*, vol. 1, pp. 135–201. North-Holland.

Hurwicz, L. (1951). "Some specification problems and applications to econometric models," *Econometrica*, 19(3), 343–344.

Keane, M. (2010). "Structural vs. atheoretic approaches to econometrics," *Journal of Econometrics*, 156, 3–20.

Khalmetski, K. (2016). "Testing guilt aversion with an exogenous shift in beliefs," *Games and Economic Behavior*, 97, 110–119.

Kimball, M. S., C. R. Sahm, and M. D. Shapiro (2008). "Imputing risk tolerance from survey responses," *Journal of the American Statistical Association*, 103(483), 1028–1038.

Klibanoff, P., M. Marinacci, and S. Mukerji (2005). "A smooth model of decision making under ambiguity," *Econometrica*, 73(6), 1849–1892.

Kothiyal, A., V. Spinu, and P. P. Wakker (2014). "An experimental test of prospect theory for predicting choice under ambiguity," *Journal of Risk and Uncertainty*, 48(1), 1–17.

Kreps, D. M., and E. L. Porteus (1978). "Temporal resolution of uncertainty and dynamic choice theory," *Econometrica:* vol. 46, 185–200.

Kube, S., M. A. Maréchal, and C. Puppe (2012). "The currency of reciprocity: Gift exchange in the workplace," *American Economic Review*, 102(4), 1644–1662.

(2013). "Do wage cuts damage work morale? Evidence from a natural field experiment," *Journal of the European Economic Association*, 11(4), 853–870.

Lever, J., M. Krzywinski, and N. Altman (2016). "Points of significance: Model selection and overfitting," *Nature Methods*, 13(9), 703–705.

Li, Q., and J. S. Racine (2007). *Nonparametric econometrics: Theory and practice.* Princeton University Press.

Low, H., and C. Meghir (2017). "The use of structural models in econometrics," *Journal of Economic Perspectives*, 31(2), 33–58.

Luce, D. (1959). *Individual choice behavior.* John Wiley.

Manski, C. F. (2002). "Identification of decision rules in experiments on simple games of proposal and response," *European Economic Review*, 46(4–5), 880–891.

(2004). "Measuring expectations," *Econometrica*, 72(5), 1329–1376.

Manski, Charles F and Molinari, Francesca. Rounding probabilistic expectations in surveys, *Journal of Business & Economic Statistics*, 28(2), 219–231.

McFadden, D., and K. Train (2000). "Mixed MNL models for discrete response," *Journal of Applied Econometrics*, 15(5), 447–470.

McLachlan, G. J., S. X. Lee, and S. I. Rathnayake (2019). "Finite mixture models," *Annual Review of Statistics and its Application*, 6, 355–378.

Nevo, A., and M. Whinston (2010). "Taking the dogma out of econometrics: Structural modeling and credible inference," *Journal of Economic Perspectives*, 24, 69–82.

Nyarko, Y., and A. Schotter (2002). "An experimental study of belief learning using elicited beliefs," *Econometrica*, 70(3), 971–1005.

Paarsch, H. J., and B. Shearer (2000). "Piece rates, fixed wages, and incentive effects: Statistical evidence from payroll records," *International Economic Review*, 41(1), 59–92.

Paarsch, H. J., and B. S. Shearer (1999). "The response of worker effort to piece rates: Evidence from the British Columbia tree-planting industry," *Journal of Human Resources*, vol. 34 643–667.

Paul Schultz, T. (2004). "School subsidies for the poor: Evaluating the Mexican Progresa poverty program," *Journal of Development Economics*, 74(1), 199–250.

Quiggin, J. (1982). "A theory of anticipated utility," *Journal of Economic Behavior and Organization*, 3(4), 323–343.

Rabin, M. (1993). "Incorporating fairness into game theory and economics," *The American Economic Review*, 1281–1302.

Revelt, D., and K. Train (1998). "Mixed logit with repeated choices: Households' choices of appliance efficiency level," *Review of Economics and Statistics*, 80(4), 647–657.

Rust, J. (2010). "Comments on: Structural vs. atheoretic approaches to econometrics by Michael Keane," *Journal of Econometrics*, 156(1), 21–24.

Shearer, B. (2004). "Piece rates, fixed wages and incentives: Evidence from a field experiment," *Review of Economic Studies*, 71, 513–534.

StataCorp, L. (2021). *Stata choice models reference manual*. Release 17 Stata Press.

Todd, P. E., and K. I. Wolpin (2006). "Assessing the impact of a school subsidy program in Mexico: Using a social experiment to validate a dynamic behavioral model of child schooling and fertility," *American Economic Review*, 96(5), 1384–1417.

Train, K. E. (1998). "Recreation demand models with taste differences over people," *Land Economics*, 230–239.

(2008). "EM algorithms for nonparametric estimation of mixing distributions," *Journal of Choice Modelling*, 1(1), 40–69.

(2009). *Discrete choice methods with simulation*. Cambridge University Press.

Von Gaudecker, H.-M., A. Van Soest, and E. Wengstrom (2011). "Heterogeneity in risky choice behavior in a broad population," *American Economic Review*, 101(2), 664–694.

Wakker, P. P. (2010). *Prospect theory: For risk and ambiguity*. Cambridge University Press.

Wik, M., T. Aragie Kebede, O. Bergland, and S. T. Holden (2004). "On the measurement of risk aversion from experimental data," *Applied Economics*, 36(21), 2443–2451.

Wilcox, N. T. (2011). "'Stochastically more risk averse:' A contextual theory of stochastic discrete choice under risk," *Journal of Econometrics*, 162(1), 89–104.

Wooldridge, J. M. (2010). *Econometric analysis of cross section and panel data*, 2nd ed. MIT Press.

Acknowledgments

This paper is based on invited lectures given over the last few years. The author thanks Sabine Kröger, editors, anonymous reviewers, students and faculty of the Universities of Zürich, Cologne, Lyon, Maastricht, Munich, Mainz and Paris for comments and suggestions.

Cambridge Elements

Behavioural and Experimental Economics

Nicolas Jacquemet
University Paris-1 Panthéon Sorbonne and the Paris School of Economics

Nicolas Jacquemet is a full professor at University Paris-1 Panthéon Sorbonne and the Paris School of Economics. His research combines experimental methods and econometrics to study discrimination, the effect of personality traits on economic behaviour, the role of social pre-involvement in strategic behaviour and experimental game theory. His research has been published in *Econometrica, Management Science, Games and Economic Behavior*, the *Journal of Environmental Economics and Management*, the *Journal of Health Economics*, and the *Journal of Economic Psychology*.

Olivier L'Haridon
Université de Rennes 1

Olivier L'Haridon is a full professor at the Université de Rennes I, France. His research combines experimental methods and decision theory, applied in the study of individual decision making as affected by uncertainty. His work has been published in *American Economic Review, Management Science*, the *Journal of Risk and Uncertainty, Theory and Decision, Experimental Economics*, the *Journal of Health Economics*, and the *Journal of Economic Psychology*.

About the Series

Cambridge Elements in Behavioural and Experimental Economics focuses on recent advances in two of the most important and innovative fields in modern economics. It aims to provide better understanding of economic behavior, choices, strategies and judgements, particularly through the design and use of laboratory experiments.

Cambridge Elements $\equiv$

Behavioural and Experimental Economics

Elements in the Series

Public Finance with Behavioural Agents
Raphaël Lardeux

*Estimation of Structural Models Using Experimental Data From the Lab
and the Field*
Charles Bellemare

A full series listing is available at: www.cambridge.org/BEE

Printed in the United States
by Baker & Taylor Publisher Services